Epic Empires

Discover the Rise and Legacy of
Powerful Islamic Dynasties in History

SARAH GULFRAZ

Copyright © 2025 Sarah Gulfraz

Sarah Gulfraz has asserted her right to be identified as the author of this Work in accordance with the Copyright, Designs and Patents Act 1988.

All rights reserved.

No portion of this book may be reproduced in any form, stored in a retrieval system, stored in a database, or published/transmitted in any form or by any means, electronic, mechanical, photocopying, recording or otherwise, without prior written permission of the publisher.

Dedication

~ Bismillah ~

May Allah (swt) accept our efforts and grant us success in this life and the next. Ameen.

In dedication to my loving family and all their support.

Contents

1. Introduction — 1
2. The Rashidun Caliphate (632–661 CE) — 6
3. The Umayyad Caliphate (661–750 CE) — 19
4. The Abbasid Caliphate (750–1258 CE) — 28
5. The Seljuk Empire (1037–1194 CE) — 38
6. The Fatimid Caliphate (909–1171 CE) — 44
7. The Mamluk Sultanate (1250–1517 CE) — 54
8. The Ottoman Empire (1299–1922 CE) — 61
9. The Mughal Empire (1526–1857 CE) — 72
10. The Safavid Empire (1501–1736 CE) — 84
11. Comparative Analysis and Legacy of Islamic Empires — 91
12. Conclusion — 95

Find Out More — 99

Chapter One

Introduction

Throughout history, Islamic empires have faced many ups and downs, shaped the course of civilisations and left marks in the form of legacies that are still contributing to continue to influence the world today. Of those, the Islamic dynasties are the most long-lasting and remarkable because their tales merge a rich tapestry of cultural, political, and scientific achievements.

The aim of Islam was to transform into a universal faith and culture stretching from one edge of the earth to the other. The initial Muslim caliphates—the Arabs, Persians, and Turks—aspired to build the classical Islamic culture. These states not only enlarged their lands but also contributed to development in management, creativity, learning, and trade that surpassed their era.

In this book we set out on an enlightening journey through the central instances and giant characters that shaped the Islamic world. Islam, which translates to universal humanism, bars bias based on race, tongue, or ethnicity, but it has some distinct traits that differentiate it from other contemporary societies.

This book will look at how these dynasties grew from humble beginnings to establish vast empires with indelible marks on the collective history of mankind. Each chapter of this book aims to detail the challenges the empires underwent, the reforms they made, and the marks—legacies—these empires left behind that continue to echo in the modern world.

The Arabian Peninsula is a huge and varied area in Southwest Asia. Its history goes back thousands of years, and many cultures and civilisations have made this region their home. The peninsula is bordered by the Red Sea to the west, the Persian Gulf to the north, and the Indian Ocean to the south. The story of Islamic dynasties begins in the Arabian Peninsula, where the Rashidun Caliphate established the foundations of a kingdom that spanned continents.

Under the leadership of the first four caliphs: Hazrat Abu Bakr (RA), Hazrat Umar (RA), Hazrat Uthman (RA), and Hazrat Ali (RA)—Islam evolved from a regional faith into a unifying force that brought diverse people together. Prophet Muhammad (PBUH) was succeeded as ruler of the Islamic empire by these four Rightly Guided Caliphs.

The early years of Islam were filled with triumphs and trials as the Rashidun Caliphs dealt with the challenges of succession, governance, and military expansion. They placed a high value on justice, consultation, and the fair distribution of resources, thereby setting a precedent for governance that would inspire future Islamic rulers.

After the Rashidun period, the Umayyad Caliphate emerged as the dominant power and expanded the borders of the Islamic world from Spain in the west to India in the east. During this period, as Islam continued to conquer, the basic social and legal structures of the emerging Islamic civilisation were established. The Umayyads were instrumental in transforming the caliphate from a religious community into a structured empire with a sophisticated administrative system.

They promoted architectural wonders such as the Great Mosque of Damascus, where Byzantine and Persian influences merged into a distinctly Islamic form. People of all ages could experience emotion, be inspired, and feel awe from these wonders. However, the Umayyads were also criticised for their departure from the egalitarian ideals of the earlier caliphs, causing discontent and ultimately leading to their downfall.

The Abbasid Caliphate, which succeeded the Umayyads, ushered in a golden age of Islamic civilisation. With Baghdad at its centre, the Abbasids ushered in an era of unprecedented intellectual and cultural prosperity. During the Abbasid Caliphate, Baghdad developed into a centre for mathematics, science, and medicine, among other things.

Because the early Islamic era saw so many scientific and artistic advances, it is often referred to as the Golden Age of Islam. The House of Wisdom became a beacon of knowledge. Legendary figures such as Al-Khwarizmi, the father of algebra, and Ibn Sina, a pioneer of medicine, illustrate the scientific achievements of this period. Despite internal turmoil and external invasions, the Abbasid legacy has persisted and influenced future generations.

As the Abbasid Caliphate waned, new Islamic dynasties emerged, leaving their unique historical imprint. The Fatimids of North Africa and Egypt distinguished themselves through their patronage of arts and architecture, evident in the construction of Al-Azhar University, one of the world's oldest institutions of learning.

The Fatimids ruled much of the Mediterranean for more than two centuries. In Spain, the Umayyads established the Caliphate of Cordoba and transformed the region into a centre of cultural and intellectual exchange. The city of Cordoba, with its magnificent mosques and vibrant libraries, is evidence of the fusion of Islamic, Christian, and Jewish traditions.

The most important Islamic empires included the Ottoman, Safavid, and Mughal empires, which made significant contributions to the geopolitical and cultural landscapes of their respective regions. The Ottoman Empire, which spanned Europe, Asia, and Africa, demonstrated exemplary administrative efficiency and military strength.

Under great leaders such as Suleiman the Magnificent, the Ottoman Empire maintained a sound legal system, outstanding architecture, and a thriving art scene. The Safavid Empire in Persia, meanwhile, established Shia Islam as a unifying identity, fostering a distinct artistic and cultural heritage exemplified by the stunning mosques of Isfahan.

In South Asia, the Mughal Empire reached unprecedented heights of splendour and cultural synthesis. The Mughal Empire ruled the Indian subcontinent for about 200 years. With an army of about a million men at arms and an economy more powerful than any other empire of the time, it grew to become one of the largest empires in the world. The Mughals created new architecture and works of art, some of which are now considered iconic images of India.

The Mughals are perhaps best remembered for their architectural achievements, including the Taj Mahal, a symbol of love and artistic excellence. In addition to architecture, the Mughals promoted advances in agriculture, trade, and governance, leaving a legacy that continues to influence the subcontinent today.

The two empires had myriad features in common, one of which made them legendary. One general feature among them was their capacity to unite people from diverse backgrounds under one religion while embracing moral relativity.

This legacy is reflected in cities such as Baghdad and Cordoba, which boast a rich Islamic heritage. Through the globalisation of different societal and political traditions, these empires cultivated diverse cultures that not only sustained but developed humanity. This diversity enabled the people within these empires to create great innovations.

Another defining feature was their emphasis on governance and justice. The importance of justice, in fact, can be traced back to the Prophet Muhammad's (PBUH) era, whereby he had himself appointed to the difficult position as the supervisor and the chief judge of every case of dispute at the earliest time. Since the Prophet's (PBUH) death, the caliphs took on the role of governance and justice.

During the period of rule, different Islamic rulers made excuses for set systems to ensure the balanced exercise of central power with local autonomy, which allowed huge and different empires to exist in harmony. The extended notion of justice transcended the treatment of non-Muslim communities, with the dhimma system making certain that these groups were often provided with protection. The term "dhimma" in Islamic law literature and prophetic traditions (ḥadith) means the duty of Muslims in general and Muslim rulers in particular to provide protection to non-Muslims residing under their authority.

It is the teaching of leadership, building cultural synthesis, and the power of resilience that an Islamic dynasty will always contribute to the modern world. Their innumerable achievements are reminders of the alliance's strength and show how important it is to build structured societies to encourage diversity.

In many ways, the stirring tales of these empires will resound for the rest of us in a time of maddening complexity, stark reminders of how human genius and cooperation can confront challenges and bring about a better world.

This book is more than the chronicles of an empire; rather, it is a challenge for you to discover how this legacy has shaped the path of civilisation prosperity in this world. It projects the leadership and cultural synthesis shown as lessons to impart on how these rulers laid the foundations of the world.

While probing the heights and traditions offered by these Islamic dynasties, we must better measure history's edge and the lasting impression carved by these civilisations. Let's begin!

Chapter Two

The Rashidun Caliphate (632-661 CE)

Foundation and Early Expansion

The new leader or organiser of the Muslim community was chosen following the death of the Prophet Muhammad (PBUH) in 632. The term "Caliph," which derives from the Arabic word "khalifah," which means "successor chosen by Allah (SWT)," was used to refer to this leader. The caliph ruled over a caliphate, a political-religious state that quickly expanded into an empire.

In Islamic history, the Rashidun Caliphate—the "Rightly Guided Caliphs"—is the name given to the first four caliphs. They were all associated with Muhammad (PBUH) and were renowned for their piety and leadership. The first four caliphs of the Islamic world were Rashidun, also referred to as the orthodox or patriarchal caliphs in Muslim history: Abu Bakr (RA) (632–634), 'Umar (RA) (634–644), 'Uthman (RA) (644–656), and 'Ali (RA) (656–661).

The Arab Peninsula was covered by the Islamic empire at the time of Prophet Muhammad's (PBUH) death. This fledgling state was set to undergo a social and religious upheaval, one of the most spectacular expansionist campaigns in history, and then political anarchy, which would ultimately lead to its downfall but would not have prevented the Islamic civilisation from solidifying its position as a preeminent cultural, political, and military force.

When Prophet Muhammad (PBUH) passed away, his followers were devastated; many even found it difficult to accept his passing. Muhammad's (PBUH) followers were now concerned that they would no longer be led by the divine force because he had professed to have received revelations from Allah (SWT). Since Muhammad (PBUH) had neither a natural heir nor an heir appointed to his post, more pragmatic concerns arose.

Apostasy, or Ridda in Arabic, refers to the declaration made by numerous Arabian tribes shortly after Muhammad's (PBUH) death. These tribes claimed that their agreement with him was personal in character and that they felt no duty to Islam. Making the situation worse, others began proclaiming themselves as prophets. The Muslims, however, saw these individuals as imposters, as Muhammad (PBUH) had made it very evident to his followers throughout his lifetime that he was the final prophet of Allah (SWT).

Therefore, leadership was crucial to maintaining unity among the Muslim community, guaranteeing leadership, and averting dissension. It extended Islam's influence, protected it from outside assaults, and upheld its doctrines. The caliphs established Sharia-based justice, government, and economic stability. Their leadership upheld unity and moral governance, setting an example for other Islamic states.

Islam's first period without the Prophet Muhammad's (PBUH) leadership lasted 29 years under the Rashidun. However, his example in both private and public life became the standard (Sunnah) for his successors, and a sizable and powerful group of Anṣār (the Prophet's (PBUH) companions)) closely monitored the caliphs to ensure they strictly adhered to the Sunnah and divine revelation (the Quran). Therefore, the Rashidun took on all of Muhammad's (PBUH) responsibilities, with the exception of prophetic duties.

The caliphate expanded from a solely Arabian power to one of the greatest empires in history during their rule. The Islamic Empire ruled over a vast region, from Egypt in the west to Persia in the east. The Islamic Empire ruled the Iranian Plateau, the Arabian Peninsula, much of North Africa, and portions of Central and South Asia in the east at the collapse of the Rashidun Caliphate in 661.

The Leadership of the First Four Caliphs

Caliph Abu Bakr RA (r. 632-634 CE)

Hazrat Abu Bakr (RA) was selected as the initial heir. One of Prophet Muhammad's (PBUH) wives, Aisha (RA), was his daughter, and he was also a very good friend of the Holy Prophet (PBUH). Hazrat Abu Bakr (RA) was a devout and moral man who had compassion for the underprivileged. By gathering information, he contributed to the defence of Mecca and the writing of the Quran.

Hazrat Abu Bakr (RA), a member of the Quraish tribe, was one of the wealthy Meccan traders. Abu Bakr (RA) had travelled to Yemen on business at the time Muhammad (PBUH) was given prophetic status. People flocked to him as soon as he returned to share the "strange" news that angel Hazrat Gabriel (AS) was giving revelations to Muhammad (PBUH). Abu Bakr (RA) was too well acquainted with the Prophet's (PBUH) honesty and truthfulness to have any doubts. Born in Mecca in AD 573 and just three years younger than the Prophet (PBUH), he had been his close friend since he was a young boy.

Abu Bakr (RA), however, went to meet the Prophet (PBUH) upon hearing about Islam and questioned him about its teachings. Without hesitation, he embraced Islam because he had unwavering faith in the Prophet (PBUH). For this reason, the Prophet (PBUH) called him As-Siddiq (the upright). As a result, he was among the Prophet's (PBUH) most ardent followers and the first man to accept Islam.

Abu Bakr's (RA) high moral standards had earned him a reputation even before Islam. He had wonderful relationships with everyone and was truthful and honest. He was trusted by the Quraish, who sought his advice on how to handle their issues. After converting to Islam, he started sharing the gospel with his social circle.

Hazrat Abu Bakr (RA) was the first ruler of the Rashidun Caliphate, ruling from 632 to 634. Known by the title "The Truthful," he played a vital role in quelling uprisings in the area and solidified the Caliphate's dominance.

His caliphate lasted for just two years, two months, and fifteen days. By conventional measures, this time frame was too brief to have a significant historical impact. Surprisingly, though, Abu Bakr's (RA) caliphate altered the entire path of history rather than just affecting it. The remarkable wonders of history include the eradication of apostasy, the reunification of Arabia, and the conquering of larger portions of Syria and Iraq in a two-year period. These campaigns' swiftness, size, scope, and durability inspire awe and adoration in us. Abu Bakr (RA) has a special place in both the history of Islam and the world because of these accomplishments.

Assuming Khalifa-tul-Rasool as his title, his leadership came to light during a period of intense hostility between the Ansar (Medinan converts) and the Muhajirun (Meccan immigrants). During a crucial meeting at Saqifah, Hazrat Umar (RA) suggested that Hazrat Abu Bakr (RA) be the leader in maintaining Islamic unity. Most Muslims, including Hazrat Ali (RA), initially hesitated and then vowed allegiance to him.

Hazrat Abu Bakr (RA) emphasised justice, truth, and obedience to Allah (SWT) and His Messenger (PBUH) in his first speech as Caliph. He also asked for guidance if he made any mistakes. During his short term, notable accomplishments were made. During the Apostasy Campaigns, he ended the Arab tribes' uprising and brought Arabia under Medina's rule. In addition, he launched operations against the Byzantine and Persian Empires, laying the groundwork for an empire that would expand quickly in the years that followed.

Preserving the Quran was one of his greatest accomplishments. Hazrat Umar (RA) persuaded Hazrat Abu Bakr (RA) to approve the compilation of the Quran after numerous memorisers were killed at the Battle of Yamama. The verses were gathered, checked, and assembled by a committee under the direction of Zayd ibn Thabit, producing a single copy that served as the foundation for following standardised versions.

Hazrat Abu Bakr's (RA) military operations increased Islam's influence. He ordered Khalid ibn al-Walid to attack the Persian Empire of the Sassanids. Together with volunteer forces, Khalid's tactics crushed early Persian opposition and achieved important wins. These wars played a crucial role in making the Rashidun Caliphate a powerful nation.

Hazrat Abu Bakr (RA) designated Hazrat Umar (RA) as his successor in a written will before his death. He died on August 23, 634, and was laid to rest next to the Prophet Muhammad (PBUH) in Aisha's home next to Al-Masjid al-Nabawi. Under his leadership, Islamic unity, governance, and growth were established.

Caliph Umar RA (r. 634-644 CE)

In roughly 615, Umar, a member of the Meccan tribe of Quraish's clan of Adi, converted to Islam after initially opposing Prophet Muhammad (PBUH). He was close to Hazrat Abu Bakr (RA), and by 622, he had become one of Prophet Muhammad's (PBUH) top advisors, travelling to Medina with Prophet Muhammad (PBUH) and other Meccan Muslims. The Holy Prophet's (PBUH) marriage to Umar's daughter Ḥafṣah in 625 affirmed his status in the state. Umar (RA) had a major role in bringing the Medinan Muslims to accept Abu Bakr as caliph and head of state after Muhammad's (PBUH) death.

Among the many powerful individuals who backed Hazrat Abu Bakr (RA) was Hazrat Umar (RA). He was also renowned for his fierce temper and uncompromising commitment to justice. Because Abu

Bakr (RA) preferred him as his successor, it was only fitting that Umar would add the word "commander of the faithful" to his title.

Hazrat Umar (RA) played a vital role in advancing Muslim culture. He oversaw the conquests of the Byzantine and Persian empires and the coronation of Abu Bakr (RA) as the first Caliph. The courageous and vivacious man who guided the Arabs from the Arabian Desert into the verdant fields of the ancient Fertile Crescent possessed three attributes: simplicity, poverty, and fairness.

His rule was characterised by numerous military victories as well as administrative achievements. During this impressive growth, Hazrat Umar (RA) established the guidelines for governing the conquered territories and maintained strict control over general policy. He was largely responsible for the eventual organisation of the Islamic empire, particularly its judicial system. He instituted the Islamic Hijri calendar, established the office of the qadi (judge), and formed the Diwan, a register of fighters' pensions that eventually developed into a strong administrative entity. Additionally, he founded the garrison cities of Basra and Kufah in Iraq and Al-Fusṭaṭ in Egypt.

The virtue of being a man, or muruwwa, as the Arabs called it, was exemplified by Hazrat Umar (RA). It suggests a number of qualities that are highly regarded and commended in Arab tribal culture, including courage, charity, practical wisdom, and honour. Hazrat Umar (RA) possessed exceptional practical knowledge. Practical learning, or phronesis as the Greeks called it, is basically the art of understanding what to do when and how to accomplish it. It includes the capacity to look forward, anticipate future events, and project the effects of a particular course of action.

During his rule, Hazrat Umar (RA) maintained his reputation as a strict, austere Puritan who resented public displays of immorality, gambling, inappropriate attire, misappropriation of state property, and abuse of authority. He believed that people in high positions should be morally equal to their elevated duties.

Numerous people consider Hazrat Umar (RA) among history's greatest political thinkers. He is frequently credited with creating the Islamic Empire. Under his direction, the empire grew at an unimaginable rate, and numerous administrative changes were implemented. After his death, Uthman (RA) ibn Affan (RA) became the third ruler of the Rashidun Caliphate.

Caliph Uthman (RA) (r. 644-656 CE)

Uthman (RA) ibn Affan (RA) and Ali ibn Abi Talib (RA) were the only two people left in Umar's (RA) final selection of an advisory council of six people (shura in Arabic) to choose his successor. Uthman (RA) was ultimately chosen to succeed him. He belonged to the wealthy Umayya party and was a close friend of Muhammad (PBUH), marrying two of the Prophet's (PBUH) daughters. He was also known as Ghani, or "the liberal," for his charitable deeds.

Born within Mecca's affluent and influential Umayyad clan, Uthman (RA) went on to become a prosperous merchant. Muhammad (PBUH) rapidly incited the Umayyads' animosity when he started preaching in Mecca in 615 CE, but Uthman (RA), the first convert of great social and economic status, welcomed Muhammad (PBUH) five years later. However, in the early years of Islamic history, Uthman (RA) played a passive role and hardly showed initiative or vigour.

Uthman's (RA) reign was not without military successes: All of Egypt was united, further territories in Persia were conquered, and Byzantine attempts to reclaim lost regions were thwarted. These victories were facilitated, in part, by the support of local populations (mostly Monophysites), who favoured Muslim governance over their former rulers due to the severe persecution they had endured.

Because of his frequent business travels, he had a wealth of knowledge about Syria and Abyssinia's history, geography, people, and culture. This knowledge was invaluable to the Muslims when they conquered these new areas in the three decades following the Prophet's (PBUH) death.

The Quran existed in various versions until Caliph 'Uthman (RA) established an authoritative recension of it. Though 'Uthman (RA) had a less assertive demeanour than his predecessor, he adhered to the same broad policies of 'Umar (RA). He carried on the conquests that had gradually expanded the Islamic empire, but the gains were now more expensive and yielded less money. To replace the loose tribe alliance that had developed under Muhammad (PBUH), Uthman (RA) attempted to establish a unified central authority. He gave members of his dynasty various provincial governorships and instituted a system of landed fiefs.

Despite his many achievements, Uthman (RA) was not as well-known to people as his prototypes had been. Costs were increasing, and other financial problems emerged (which Umar (RA) had managed to keep under control). The continuous expense of warfare placed a heavy burden on the Arab population, leading to widespread frustration and dissatisfaction.

In addition to being criticised for elevating his own family—who were members of the Umayya tribe—to important posts, Uthman (RA) was also charged with sacrilege. This charge was denied after his collapse. His waning popularity and his hesitation to use force against those who started to oppose him (something he might have done successfully) on the pretext that he would not shed Muslim blood ultimately led to his downfall.

So Uthman (RA), the third Rashidun caliph, faced criticism for alleged nepotism and favouritism toward his Umayyad relatives. Uthman (RA) was assassinated by rebels in 656 CE, leading to chaos and division within the Muslim community. After Uthman's assassination, Ali ibn Abi Talib became the fourth caliph.

Caliph Ali (RA) (r. 656-661 CE)

Ali (RA) was born in Mecca in 601 CE inside the sacred Kaaba. He was the son of the Islamic Prophet Muhammad's (PBUH) uncle, Abu Talib ibn Abd al-Muttalib (c. 535–619 CE), the head of the Hashim tribe. The

Prophet (PBUH), who had been orphaned at a young age, was raised by his father as though he were his son and a similar bond was formed between Ali (RA) and the Prophet (PBUH).

Ali (RA) was taken into Muhammad's (PBUH) home and developed a close relationship with him at a young age. Ali was one of the first people to embrace the new faith when Muhammad (PBUH) proclaimed his prophetic status in 610 CE (who was the first male convert is up for question, but Ali (RA) was one of the contenders). He stayed faithful to him even under the most trying circumstances.

Ali (RA), who had remained in the background until then and informed his superiors about the state issue, became the next caliph. However, his caliphate faced immediate opposition, particularly from Muawiya ibn Abi Sufyan, the governor of Syria and a relative of Uthman. After Caliph Uthman (RA) was killed, the First Fitna (civil war) broke out. Muawiya was one of the main opponents of the Rashidun Caliphate.

Despite these challenges, Ali (RA) remained steadfast in his commitment to justice and tried to bring unity to the fractured Muslim community. His leadership, though contested, is remembered for his wisdom and piety.

Overall Reforms and Governance by the Rashidun Caliphs

A state's institutionally organised governmental apparatus must be reorganised and restructured for effective "crisis management" to achieve development. Reforms and governance, which encompass the arts and science of administration and politics, are integral to administrative restructuring.

In Islam's history, governance has taken many distinct forms. Under the influence of Islamic principles and the necessity of fast growth, the most inventive application of Arab tribal norms occurred during the formative period.

Following the conquests, the ruling class added many institutions and customs from the neighbouring empires, especially the Persian Empire, to their Arab tribal system of government. The Abbasids reigned as Persian emperors, whereas the Umayyads ruled as Arab chiefs. The Rashidun Caliphate lasted for 29 years and was a crucial period in Islamic history. It was Islam's first time governing and leading without our beloved Holy Prophet Muhammad (PBUH) present.

The early Islamic state saw significant political and geographic expansion during this time. The early development of Muslim society was shaped by the caliphs' leadership, which was distinguished by a special fusion of practical governance and spiritual teaching. According to the teachings of the Prophet Muhammad (PBUH), they designed an Islamic society founded on equality, justice, and fairness. Historical reforms not only succeeded in ending the current problems but also left a legacy of moral leadership and social balance that continues to shape discussions about governance today. Let's have a look at the details.

Abu Bakr's (RA) uncompromising dedication to Islamic values, humility, and profound piety characterised his leadership. One of his greatest accomplishments was commissioning the Quran's compilation, which guaranteed the sacred book's survival for upcoming generations. He showed how crucial it is to uphold Islamic values while handling difficult political situations. As a democratic leader of the Islamic community, he sought advice from distinguished friends on all significant issues. Despite his short term, he established a high bar for caliphal leadership.

Under Umar's (RA) era, significant reforms that had a long-lasting effect on the Islamic government were implemented. He instituted several social welfare programs, created the Islamic calendar, and established a formal administrative framework. Umar (RA) also established new military, justice, schooling, finance agencies and institutions. In addition, he imposed new levies, including zakat on horse ownership and Ushr, a commercial tax on non-Muslim traders.

Umar (RA) also established a large portion of the administrative framework. It was up to Umar (RA) to make the empire function, although his predecessor's brief rule was characterised by constant conflict and chaos, which he was able to handle. His key administrative accomplishments include:

- The establishment of provinces in newly conquered territories
- The appointments of governors to oversee those provinces
- The creation of a revenue office to oversee finances and formalise the state treasury
- The creation of a robust and autonomous judicial system
- The implementation of pensions for troops rather than allocating the captured territory to them
- The implementation of changes in the military to maintain discipline and discourage cowardice
- The establishment of a night watch, which subsequently evolved into a police or municipal guard system.

Following his patriarch's example, Umar (RA) divided the acquired territory into multiple smaller provinces for efficient administration, even though the empire had already been divided into different provinces during the Prophet's (PBUH) lifetime. Umar (RA) is praised for his extensive changes and efficient and just rule. He is renowned for founding Medina as the first Islamic city and enacting several administrative, social, and economic reforms that served as the cornerstone for the growth of Islamic civilisation.

The Islamic empire continued to grow during the Uthman (RA) caliphate, eventually reaching India in the east and Spain in the west. Additionally, he was responsible for compiling the Quran into a single, uniform text. But dissension and controversy dogged his reign.

Political upheaval and internal dissension characterised Uthman (RA)'s tenure, and his administration came under fire for alleged favouritism. Tribal unrest increased during his final four years, and his expulsion of collaborators exacerbated the rift. Ali's (RA) name was used by Yemeni Jew Abdullah bin Saba to stir up conflict and divide Muslim society into groups. Although these nominations were made based on loyalty and merit, Uthman (RA) was also charged with nepotism for selecting family members as governors. Notwithstanding these difficulties, his rule also witnessed important developments in public infrastructure, including wells and roads, and the growth of the Islamic empire through victories in North Africa and Cyprus.

Several wars and crises characterised Ali's (RA) caliphate, notably an uprising headed by Muawiyah ibn Abi Sufyan, the governor of Syria. Ali and Muawiyah's dispute ultimately resulted in the Battle of Siffin, which was indecisive and gave rise to the Kharijites, who disapproved of Ali and Muawiyah. Addressing the political and social instability that followed Uthman (RA)'s murder was the main goal of his rule. He was renowned for his legal judgements and extraordinary understanding of the Quran. He was a key contributor to the Quran's compilation and the establishment of Islamic jurisprudence.

Ali (RA) was an influential figure in the development of Islamic jurisprudence and was firmly committed to justice. Throughout his tenure as leader, there were many major confrontations.Despite these obstacles, Ali's (RA) services to Islamic law and thought continue to have a significant impact, demonstrating his commitment to fairness and justice.

The Rashidun Caliphate's Transition

Ali's (RA) assassination in 661 CE brought an end to the Rashidun Caliphate, and the Islamic community saw a dramatic change in leadership. Hasan, the son of Ali (RA), briefly took over but abdicated to stop more carnage, opening the door for Muawiya I's Umayyad Caliphate. The demand for a more stable government in the face of growing factionalism led to this change from Rashidun's elective administration to a hereditary monarchy. The future of the Islamic government was shaped by the Rashidun heritage of justice and group decision-making, which stood in stark contrast to the autocratic character of Umayyad power.

In conclusion, the "Rightly Guided Caliphs," also known as al-Khulafaaal-Rashidun, were instrumental in forming Islamic culture and history. They were renowned for their piety, leadership, and commitment to Islam. Each of the four caliphs significantly aided the advancement of Islamic civilisation.

Chapter Three

The Umayyad Caliphate (661-750 CE)

Rise and Consolidation of Power

For the history of Islam and the Middle East, 661–750 AD were pivotal. From Syria, the Muslim-conquered regions of the Middle East, North Africa, and Spain were governed by a line of caliphs from the Umayyad family, the first caliph dynasty in Islamic history.

They led a changeover of the region during their reign and Islam's classical creation as a religion and civilisation. The caliphate was a world of fast growth during the Umayyads. The Islamic Caliphate, one of the smallest combined powers in history, was one of the few to directly control three civilisations (Africa, Europe and Asia).

The Iberian Peninsula (Al-Andalus), the Maghreb, Sindh, the Caucasus, and Transoxia were all included in the Muslim world by the Umayyads. With 62 million inhabitants (29% of the world's population) and an area of 5.79 million square miles at its height, the Umayyad Caliphate was the fifth-largest empire in history in terms of both population and size.

Uthman (RA)'s Rule, Rebellion, and the Ascension of Ali

But back in the Arabian Peninsula, as the Caliph, Uthman (RA) had a more pronounced nepotism, which did not endear him well to some of the people of Quraish. It was actually because this tribe of the Umayyad started getting employment in administrative and official capacities, which made other tribes of the Quraish feel neglected, like in the case of Muawiya in Syria.

Prophet Muhammad's (PBUH) widow, Ayesha (RA), also started to speak ill of Uthman (RA) regarding his style of governance and even the way he understood Islam. An uprising against him was felt in Egypt and Iraq and was instigated by the annoyed tribes of the Quraish.

When the Egyptian rebels arrived, the negotiations between the parties were in progress, and the partisans of Uthman (RA) guaranteed they would soon make reparations to the Egyptian rebels. While returning, however, the rebels captured a letter from Uthman (RA) to the Egyptian governor, who told them that upon their return home, he would kill them.

Outraged, the rebels turned back to Medina and laid siege to Uthman (RA) in his home. This time, the crowd demanded nothing more than a new caliph. Two days into the siege, rioting broke out that set the Caliph's house on fire and killed some of his defenders. At the time of midday prayers, two Egyptians found their way over the walls of Uthman (RA)'s home and killed him. Uthman (RA)'s house was looted.

It appeared that the Umayyad state had disappeared. The people looked towards the only living male relative of the Prophet Muhammad (PBUH). This was Ali ibn Abi Talib, who was related to the Prophet Muhammad (PBUH) as his cousin and husband of his daughter Hazrat Fatima (RA). Ali (RA) was an early follower of the Prophet (PBUH), a warrior in his army, and married his daughter.

In Shia Islam (Shia is the word for Party, meaning the Party of Ali (RA)), Ali (RA) was considered the rightful successor after Muhammad (PBUH) was gone. Aisha and other atabi went back to their homes discouraged, but Ali (RA) seemed to be the best candidate for Caliph after the Qureshi power slipped from his hands following the Prophet's (PBUH) death (PBUH), which became apparent when Uthman (RA) was assassinated in 656.

Ali (RA), however, appears to have turned down this offer. After all, he would have had to take over the Muslim community during a time of turmoil; the last two Caliphs had short terms that ended in assassination. Nevertheless, after some deliberation, Ali (RA) accepted the role.

In the holy month of al-Hijjah in the Muslim calendar, Muslims across Medina came to swear allegiance to him. Unlike his forbears, Ali's (RA) power base was not in the Arabian Peninsula. While the Caliphs Abu Bakr, Umar, and Uthman (RA) ruled from Mecca and Medina, the cities where Islam had begun, Ali moved his capital to Kufa in Iraq.

He had accumulated the support he had gained during his years of exile, which were years that he spent out of favour with the Quraish of Mecca. The issue that emerged was that he now governed a bigger Muslim community in which the family of Uthman, the Umayyad tribe, dominated most of the regional power outside Iraq. Ali (RA) fought against this. He removed virtually all Uthman (RA) appointed governors, alleging they were corrupt. This comprised the influential Muawiya in Syria. Muawiya had no friendly response to the orders from Ali (RA).

The Transition from the Rashidun to the Umayyad Caliphate under Muawiya I

Arab Muslims controlled one of the world's largest empires by the end of the seventh century CE. They had no idea how to manage the vast and diversified people. The empire supplied enough resources to maintain everyone's happiness as long as it grew. However, it faltered when it stopped expanding.

The term "First Fitna" describes the first significant civil war in the Islamic world, which broke out between 656 and 661 CE after Uthman ibn Affan, the third caliph, was assassinated. Because it caused divides among the Muslim community and paved the way for the rise of several groups, most notably the Sunni and Shia branches of Islam, this battle represented a crucial turning point in Islamic history. Several significant engagements occurred throughout the conflict, the most famous of which was the Battle of Siffin in 657 CE.

Because Ali was unable to bring the killings to justice, Muawiyah refused to recognise him as caliph. By personally utilising the state treasury for espionage and purchasing people's allegiance, the disobedient Muawiya persisted in transgressing Islamic precepts. Syria's populace completely trusted him and the misleading narrative he painted. Ali dispatched Jarir, an ambassador, to Syria to find a diplomatic solution and prevent violence. Although the negotiations failed, Jarir reported back that Muawiyah would comply once the killers were apprehended.

After initially preparing to invade Syria from the north, Imam Ali (RA) launched a direct attack by marching across the Mesopotamian desert after realising that war was unavoidable. When they arrived in Riqqa, they discovered that the locals were hostile towards Imam Ali (RA). As a result, his army had a tough time crossing the river, but they could do so by using a bridge made of boats. The troops of Imam Ali ibn Abi Talib (RA) finally caught sight of Muawiya's major forces, who were stationed on the river plain at Siffin in ZilHijjah 36 A.H. (May 657).

Muawiyah observed from a pavilion as Ali personally commanded his Medinan men, preferring to let his officer Amr ibn al-Aas lead the conflict. Amr ibn al-Aas burst through a portion of the opposing line at one point and almost killed Ali. In response, Malik ibn Ashter launched a fierce attack that severely damaged Muawiyah's personal guards and almost drove him from the pitch. Although Ali's soldiers suffered more casualties, the battle lasted three days, and neither side obtained the upper hand. Muawiyah, worried that he could lose, proposed to arbitrate their disagreements.

The army turned down Imam Ali's (RA) requests for representatives in the arbitration, including Abdullah ibn Abbas and Malik al-Ashtar. Muawiyah was adamantly opposed to al-Ashtar since he was a regicide and would have had him put to death. Additionally, Abdullah was directly related to Imam Ali (RA) and hence strongly associated with his cause. Because of this, the soldiers feared that these individuals would push Imam Ali's (RA) claims too hard and be unwilling to make concessions, prolonging the conflict.

Therefore, the men of Imam Ali (RA) demanded that Abu Musa al-Ash'ari be selected as his representative. Abu Musa, a Bedouin like most of the soldiers, was believed to be genuinely dedicated to peace. Nevertheless, he had previously abandoned Imam Ali (RA), and his commitment to him was dubious. Amr al-Aas, Muawiya's general, was chosen to act as his spokesperson. Muawiyah went to Damascus, while Imam Ali (RA) retreated to Kufa.

This meant that even if Imam Ali (RA) had won the real battle, Muawiyah still held the advantage. Imam Ali (RA) had been denied the opportunity to select his own agent in the dispute resolution. The peace pact did not acknowledge him as Caliph but positioned both him and Muawiyah as equal warring parties. Furthermore, the arbitration was scheduled for several months after the fight; had it occurred sooner, Imam Ali (RA) might have resumed the conflict if he had found the decision unsatisfactory.

Because they believed that the arbitration was improper under Islam, Imam Ali's (RA) adherents seceded from the main army. Although it was only temporary, Imam Ali (RA) was able to calm these men and convince them to rejoin his army. Later, the Kharijites (dissenters) were centred on these warriors. Imam Ali (RA) ruled the remainder of the Muslim Empire during the arbitration, while Muawiyah ruled Syria. The status quo was maintained after the arbitration failed. While

Muawiyah ruled Egypt and Syria, sustaining hostilities, Imam Ali (RA) continued to be recognised as Caliph. Muawiyah, who was crowned in Jerusalem, founded the Umayyad caliphate and set about enlarging it.

The Battle of Nahrawan and the Tragic End of Ali's Leadership

This was the battle of Nahrawan. Ali (RA) fought against an alliance of his critics, known as the Kharijites (Arabic for those who had "gone out" or "rebelled"). The Kharijites were a particularly violent group known to interrogate and execute civilians on their campaign trail, depending on their views on Uthman (RA) and Ali (RA).

The battle of Nahrawan was a significant victory for Ali (RA). His army was superior in both strength and numbers. The Kharijite army was almost entirely wiped out, with the few survivors pardoned by Ali (RA). However, Ali (RA)'s success against the Kharijite army would return to haunt him. Members of his own following, still sympathetic to the Kharijite cause, began to defect secretly to Muawiya, the Umayyad governor of Syria.

Ali (RA) was ultimately assassinated while at prayer in the Great Mosque of Kufa, Iraq. His murderer, an Egyptian Kharijite named Ibn Muljam, stabbed Ali (RA) with a poisoned sword. As the last of the four Rightly Guided Caliphs, Ali (RA) succumbed to his wounds two days later. His death marked another shift in the centre of Muslim power—having already moved from Medina to Kufa in Iraq. Upon his death, the seat of the caliphate moved from Kufa to Damascus in Syria.

The man who now held all the power was none other than Muawiyah of the Umayyad tribe. Hearing of Ali (RA)'s death, Muawiyah marched his army to Kufa, which he entered during the summer. There, he was recognised by the Iraqi Muslim community after issuing an ultimatum: they had three days to accept his authority or face death.

Ali (RA)'s son, Hasan, initially succeeded his father. However, after some dispute and preparation for war, Hasan abdicated in favour of Muawiyah in exchange for compensation. Hasan lived until his death in 670, reportedly due to poisoning allegedly ordered by Muawiyah.

With Ali (RA)'s demise and Hasan's abdication, the new Umayyad caliphate, Muawiyah, resumed the challenging task of governing the Levant's diverse religious and tribal makeup. Earlier in his career, Muawiyah had conquered large portions of the predominantly Christian Byzantine Empire.

Muawiyah now ruled these people in a careful balance of friendship and cooperation with local tribal leaders. His army was engaged in almost yearly campaigns against the Christian Byzantine Empire, which secured a steady loot income. Loyalty to Muwaiyah's rule in Iraq remained fragile as many there continued to demonstrate support for the deceased Ali (RA) and even the strict religious practices of the Kharijites.

As in Syria, Muawiyah relied on local leaders to govern on his behalf and formed good relations with the leaders of the Thaqif tribe, to whom he gave a great deal of independence in return for loyalty. As in the civil war with Ali (RA), Muawiyah proved to be a clever leader who relied on carefully cultivated networks of loyal followers to consolidate his rule. However, the biggest shift from his predecessors came in 676 when he appointed his son Yazid to succeed him. The creation of a dynasty was seen as illegitimate in the Islamic world and caused another civil war – this is referred to as the Second Fitna by Muslims.

While Uthman (RA) had appointed his fellow tribesmen to strategic positions, no caliph before Muawiyah had institutionalised the leadership as hereditary. Yazid, on the ascendance of his father Muawiyah in 680, received a number of threats to his rightful succession. In Iraq, Ali's (RA) son, Husayn—the only grandson of the Prophet Muhammad (PBUH)—rebelled against the Umayyad Dynasty.

Rather than negotiating, the local governor attacked Husayn, leading to a clash between Husayn's followers and the local governor's army at the site known as the Battle of Karbala. Husayn was killed, marking the tragic end of the Prophet Muhammad's (PBUH) dynasty—a moment that remains highly important to this very day.

This event holds deep religious importance for Shia Muslims up to this present time. The second revolt originated from the progeny of Caliph Abu Bakr (RA), led by Ibn al-Zubayr, who revolted in Mecca on the Arabian Peninsula, establishing his control over the city. In response, Yazid's forces marched through the Arabian Peninsula, plundering Medina before besieging Ibn al-Zubayr in Mecca.

Yazid's army attacked the Kaaba, even setting fire to the black cloth known as the Kiswa. This siege came to a halt, however, when Yazid, who had ordered the siege, died in 683 under unclear circumstances. Seizing the moment, Ibn al-Zubayr proclaimed himself the new caliph, further complicating the struggle for power.

Yazid was succeeded by his son Muawiyah II, who made the Umayyads rule from the north. However, his reign was short-lived due to illness, and he died in 684 without a direct heir. From this low point, another Umayyad was once more elected as Caliph by the tribal chiefs in Syria.

This man, Marwan ibn al-Hakam, rallied the Syrian forces against his rival, Ibn al-Zubayr, and forced Ibn al-Zubayr's governor out of Egypt in 685. Marwan's son, Abd al-Malik, reclaimed territory in Iraq for the Umayyads, scoring a victory at the Battle of Maskin in 691 against Ibn al-Zubayr's brother, Mus'ab.

The following year, in 692, a pro-Umayyad army commander laid siege to Mecca once more and put an end to Ibn al-Zubayr. Finally, the Caliphate was reunified under a single Caliph: the Umayyad Abd al-Malik, who ruled from Damascus.

The Umayyad Caliphate went on to rule the Islamic world for another half-century. At its height, it ruled an area of over 4 million square miles, making it one of the largest empires in history. Under its rule, key cities in Syria, such as Damascus and Aleppo, thrived with new buildings and magnificent architecture. The Caliphate rubbed shoulders with the Christian Byzantine Empire, with whom it fought but also traded, and many Christians held prominent positions in the Umayyad court at various times during the Caliphate's life span.

The Umayyad Caliphate was a transformative and turbulent period in Islamic history. It stands as both a lesson in the complexities of governance and a testament to the enduring resilience of Islamic civilisation. Its legacy, shaped by remarkable growth and profound challenges, reminds us of the dynamic interplay of politics, religion, and culture in shaping history.

Chapter Four

The Abbasid Caliphate (750-1258 CE)

Founding and Golden Age

In the 8th century Middle East, a new dynasty seized control of one of the world's greatest empires–the Islamic Caliphate. With its numerous scientific, literary, and cultural accomplishments, the Abbasid caliphate (750–1258) has long been acknowledged as the nascent era of Islamic civilisation.

From the Abbasid caliphate's establishment in 750 and its heyday under Harun al-Rashid to the Mongol destruction of Baghdad in 1258, this history explores the caliphate's role as an institution and empire as well as its impact on Islamic society and culture. It has come to be remembered as Islam's 'golden age'. Let's have a look at the story of the Abbasid Caliphate.

The Abbasid Rise to Power and the Establishment of the New Caliphate

The Abbasids arrived in 750, less than a century and a half into Islamic history. This occurred less than half a century after the Prophet's (PBUH) time (610–632), the period of rule of his Companion substitutes (the Rashidun caliphs, 632–661), and the Islamic conquests with the Umayyad dynasty (661–750).

Hence, the Abbasids overthrew the Umayyad Empire because they set themselves apart from the Umayyads by criticising their governance and moral fibre. They particularly catered to non-Arab Muslims, who were viewed as an inferior class inside the Umayyad Empire and were excluded from the Arabs' kinship-based culture.

The Islamic empire comprised various older groups, including Arabs, Persians, Zoroastrians, Manicheans, Jews, Christians and Buddhists. These groups all contributed to the transition from the divided world of Late Antiquity, which was straddling a border along the Euphrates River between the Roman (Byzantine) and Persian (Sasanid) empires, to a single world of economic and cultural synthesis under the caliphate.

The Umayyad Dynasty, based in Damascus, Syria, was overthrown by the Abbasid Dynasty. The Persians, who coexisted with Arabs in the east and were incensed at the favour extended to Syrian Arabs, were the largest group of mawali. They were ready to rebel together.

The Umayyads infuriated other Muslims by transforming the caliphate into a hereditary succession. Some people thought that only one family should be in charge, while Shi'ites believed that the Prophet Muhammad's (PBUH) family, through his son-in-law Ali (RA), should have real power and that the Umayyads were not related to Muhammad (PBUH).

Because the Abbasids claimed to be descended from Muhammad (PBUH) through Muhammad's (PBUH) uncle Abbas, they were able to win over Shi'ites. Shi'ites would have preferred that they were descended from Muhammad (PBUH) through Ali (RA), but they still regarded the Abbasids as superior to the Umayyads. This way, following their triumph over the Umayyads, the "Abbasids" in the Middle East over these centuries converted the Umayyads' Arab empire into a multiethnic Muslim empire.

Cultural, Scientific, and Economic Achievements during the Abbasid Golden Age

The Abbasids promised a return to 'true Islam,' correcting teachings and moral leadership, and sent missionaries and agents across the Caliphate to spread their message. In eastern Khorasan, a general named Abu Muslim, likely a Persian convert, launched a revolt and took the black banner of the Hashemites as his symbol. The Hashemites, descendants of Hashim and the extended family of the Prophet (PBUH), included the Abbasids prominently among their ranks. This frontier region—comprising parts of present-day northeastern Iran, Turkmenistan, and Afghanistan—is particularly ripe for rebellion.

Arabs and non-Arab converts lived side by side, intermarrying and fighting to defend the frontier. Many viewed the Umayyads as distant and unpopular overlords. For decades, opposition stoked by Hashemite agents and missionaries seeking to topple the Umayyads sowed the seeds of revolution.

When Abu Muslim began his revolt, he quickly attracted followers—Arabs, Persians, and Central Asians, many of whom were experienced warriors. He proved to be a brilliant commander, won a series of victories over Umayyad forces and occupied Kufa, the capital of Iraq. The Abbasids assumed leadership of the revolution, and their forces eventually met the army of the Umayyad Caliph Marwan II at the Zab River.

Caliph Marwan was a courageous but rash leader. He attacked the Abbasid line with a frontal cavalry charge. The charge ended in disaster, according to Abbasid historians, when their own warriors, emboldened by their previous triumphs, built walls of spears and repelled the cavalry. Marwan himself left the battle, the Umayyads' army was crushed, and their morale was destroyed. However, he was hunted down and executed in Egypt. They also tracked down and killed other Umayyads. They even desecrated their tombs. However, one member of the dynasty, Abd al-Rahman, escaped to Spain and established the Emirate of Cordoba, which flourished in Iberia for centuries.

In the meantime, Abu-l-Abbas al-Saffah became the first Abbasid Caliph, but it took more than a decade for the Abbasids to consolidate their power. Al-Saffah moved the Caliph's residence from Harran to Kufa, closer to the Abbasid power based in Persia. In 751, he sent an army to curb the westward expansion of the Chinese Tang Dynasty, culminating in a bloody victory at the Battle of Talas, which also marked the limit of the Caliphate's eastward expansion.

Many who had helped overthrow the Umayyads sought an end to hereditary rule and a return to caliphs elected from within an elite group, but they were disappointed. Al-Saffah was succeeded by his brother al-Mansur, who became one of the greatest Abbasid caliphs.

However, al-Mansur's reign began with the execution of the brilliant and popular general Abu Muslim, who was deemed a potentially dangerous rival. He also faced rebellion from the Alids, a powerful clan descended from the Prophet's son-in-law, Ali (RA). The Alids pressed their own claim to rule. Al-Mansur crushed the last major Alid revolt, ushering in an era of stability, prosperity, and peace.

During this time, al-Mansur ordered the construction of a new capital on the banks of the Tigris River. Officially known as Madīnat as-Salām, the 'City of Peace,' the city became one of the glories of the medieval world: Baghdad.

Governance and Administration

Under the reign of al-Mansur's grandson, Harun al-Rashid, the Caliphate flourished as never before, with Baghdad at its heart. Caliph Harun al-Rashid was known as "the Rightly Guided." He was a central figure in One Thousand and One Nights, the masterpiece of Arabic literature. This represented al-Rashid as a devout, wise, and beneficent ruler who prayed 100 times a day and gave 1,000 dirhams to good causes each morning.

Al-Rashid wandered the streets of Baghdad disguised as a beggar to observe how his subjects lived. He was known as a brilliant horseman, a patron of the arts, and a keen chess player. His court was a space where even women occasionally argued and debated religion and philosophy openly.

In the Caliphate, as in much of the medieval world, few women held high status in their own right. Yet, as mothers, wives, and concubines, they could wield significant influence. Al-Khayzuran, once a Yemeni slave girl, rose from concubine to caliph's wife and exerted great power during the reigns of her husband, Caliph al-Mahdi, and her son, Caliph al-Rashid.

Renowned for her intelligence and learning, she held discussions on policy and military strategy, received foreign ambassadors, and intervened in matters of justice. Much of her vast wealth was dedicated to public works and charity. Many considered her a co-ruler or even "the real Caliph."

The success of al-Rashid's reign was underpinned by efficient governance, modelled in part on the administration of their Sassanid predecessors. Persian and Central Asian bureaucrats played a key role, notably the Barmakid family. Descended from high priests of the Buddhist temple of Nawbahar near Balkh, in modern Afghanistan, the Barmakids became influential allies of the Abbasids, shaping an age of Islamic statecraft infused with elements of Sassanian Persian culture.

They served the Abbasids faithfully for three generations, but the court's power dynamics were perilous. In 803, al-Rashid abruptly turned against the Barmakids, leading to their dramatic fall from favour, with many imprisoned or executed. Their downfall marked the end of Barmakid's control over the post of vizier, a pivotal position as the Caliph's senior advisor and chief minister. Over time, some viziers wielded so much power that they overshadowed the Caliph.

The fame of al-Rashid's court extended across the known world. Charlemagne, King of the Franks and Holy Roman Emperor, sent several embassies to Baghdad. In return, al-Rashid sent him magnificent gifts, including perfume, ivory chessboards, a marvellous water clock, and even an elephant named Abul-Abbas, who lived for several years at Charlemagne's court in Aachen.

Cultural life in the Caliphate, particularly in Baghdad, was remarkably cosmopolitan. The Abbasid court celebrated Persian holidays such as Nowruz, the Persian New Year. This openness helped the Caliphate flourish as a centre of culture, science, arts, and medicine.

The House of Wisdom, or Bayt al-Hikmah, was a renowned library in Baghdad, though little is known of its exact functions today. Across the Caliphate, scholars translated classical works from Greek, Middle Persian, and Sanskrit into Arabic. Their efforts preserved countless works by figures such as Aristotle and Galen that might otherwise have been lost. These scholars also made significant original contributions, creating knowledge that was later highly sought after by the medieval West.

Baghdad's scholars led the world in many fields. Al-Kindi, known as "the Philosopher of the Arabs," was a celebrated polymath who wrote on topics ranging from logic and psychology to astronomy and astrology. Al-Khwarizmi's contributions to mathematics earned him the title "Father of Algebra," and his Latinized name, Algorismus, is the origin of the word "algorithm." The Christian scholar Hunayn ibn Ishaq, nicknamed "the Sheikh of Translators," played a crucial role in translating ancient texts into Arabic.

Material culture thrived under the Abbasids, with innovations such as glazed pottery in the 9th century enabling new artistic expressions. Many vibrant pieces decorated with animals and Kufic lettering have been uncovered across the former Caliphate from this era. The Abbasid Caliphate also prospered from its position along the Silk Roads, the ancient trade routes linking Europe and Asia. Valuable imports travelled these routes, including silk, spices, ivory, gemstones, and thoroughbred horses. To encourage trade, the Abbasids constructed roads, inns, hospices, and wells for travellers.

Alongside goods, new ideas and technologies also flowed along the Silk Roads. For instance, Chinese papermaking techniques reached the Muslim world under the Umayyads but truly flourished under the Abbasids. Paper, much cheaper than parchment, revolutionised administration and book-making, helping medieval Islam become one of the most bookish cultures in history.

Role of Baghdad as a Cultural and Intellectual Centre

In the 7th century, the first Arab conquests pushed the frontier of the Eastern Roman Empire back to the Taurus Mountains. Since then, the Caliphate and Empire remained in a state of near-constant war, with frequent raids by both sides across the Syrian frontier. The Arabs twice besieged Constantinople but failed to capture the great city. Al-Rashid led an Abbasid force as far as the shores of the Bosphorus. By the early 9th century, the Eastern Roman Empire paid annual tribute to the Caliphate.

When Emperor Nikerphoros halted these payments, an Abbasid army crossed the Taurus Mountains and surprised his forces at Krasos. The Romans suffered a severe defeat, with the Emperor narrowly escaping. The pattern of raids and counter-raids persisted, with al-Rashid moving the Abbasid capital to Raqqa to be closer to the frontier. This focus on the West blinded the Caliph to brewing unrest in the East.

News of revolt in Khorasan reached the Caliph, and while travelling to quell the rebellion, Harun al-Rashid fell ill and died. His reign, later celebrated as a golden age for the Abbasid Caliphate, marked a period of prosperity, stability, and cultural achievement. However, his succession arrangements sowed the seeds of civil strife.

Al-Rashid designated his son Muhammad as his heir, while another son, Abdullah, was named his successor. Upon al-Rashid's death,

Muhammad became Caliph al-Amin, and Abdullah became governor of Khorasan with the title al-Ma'mun. Rival factions emerged, and al-Amin, under the influence of his advisors, annulled his father's arrangements. Furious, al-Ma'mun declared war.

The civil war culminated in al-Ma'mun's forces defeating al-Amin's army and besieging Baghdad. After a year-long siege, the city fell, and al-Amin was executed. Al-Ma'mun ruled initially from Merv, where he sought to broaden his support by allying with the Alids, descendants of Ali. This alliance, marked by symbolic gestures such as adopting green attire, eventually led to revolts in Iraq. Al-Ma'mun returned to Baghdad and abandoned the Alid alliance.

His attempts to impose a new religious doctrine further destabilised the Caliphate. The Mihna, a period of religious persecution, saw dissenting scholars imprisoned or executed. Al-Ma'mun was succeeded by al-Mu'tasim, who prioritised military reforms over theological debates.

The Abbasid armies, renowned for their prowess, included troops from diverse backgrounds. The Khorasan, known for their skill in armoured combat, formed the core of the caliph's army. Other notable contingents included the Daylam, expert skirmishers from northern Persia, and African heavy infantry armed with shields, swords, and spears.

The Abbasid armies excelled in siege warfare, employing catapults, mangonels, and naphtha-based fire weapons. Under al-Mu'tasim, a military transformation began with the recruitment of Turkish slave soldiers. Trained in both military tactics and Islamic teachings, these mamluks became elite cavalry and archers loyal to the caliph.

The rise of Turkish officers disrupted traditional military structures and angered the old nobility, many of whom lost their privileges. To mitigate tensions, al-Mu'tasim built Samarra, a city for the Turkish military elite, where grand projects like the world's largest mosque were initiated.

Despite internal tensions, al-Mu'tasim's new army achieved a significant victory against the Byzantine Empire, capturing and sacking Amorium. However, the reliance on slave soldiers eroded centuries of military tradition and foreshadowed future instability within the Caliphate.

Anarchy and the Decline of Abbasid Authority

Al-Mu'tasim was succeeded by his eldest son, al-Wathiq. After his unexpected death, another son, al-Mutawakkil, ascended to the throne with the support of Turkish generals. They anticipated a compliant figurehead, but al-Mutawakkil sought to reassert caliphal authority. Under his orders, several Turkish leaders were eliminated, and he attempted to counter their influence by employing Arab and Armenian troops.

The Turks retaliated, and al-Mutawakkil was assassinated by his own bodyguards. The ensuing chaos and civil war became known as the 'Decade of Anarchy.' Four caliphs rose to power, each controlled by the Turkish military elite and violently overthrown. Order was only restored with the accession of Caliph al-Mu'tamid, but the anarchy had severely diminished the caliph's authority.

Even before the Abbasids assumed power, maintaining control over the vast Caliphate was challenging. In the West of Egypt, the Abbasid authority was largely symbolic. The period saw multiple major uprisings as local governors and warlords claimed autonomy. Egypt, fertile and prosperous, was among the first regions lost to a rebel Turkish commander who established the Tulunid dynasty.

In southern Iraq, agricultural slaves from eastern Africa, known as the Zanj, launched a significant revolt that lasted 14 years. The revolt devastated the region, disrupted Abbasid tax revenues, and threatened Baghdad's food supply. Meanwhile, in Afghanistan, a coppersmith named Ya'qub al-Saffar rose to prominence, founding the Saffarid dynasty and conquering much of eastern Persia before being halted at the Battle of Dayr al-'Aqul.

Amid these turbulent times, Abbasid caliphs struggled to assert their authority but achieved some successes. Caliph al-Mu'tadid managed a brief resurgence through military campaigns and strategic alliances, including his marriage to Qatr al-Nada, the daughter of the Tulunid ruler of Egypt. Renowned for her intelligence and poise, she was described as one of the most remarkable women of her time. Her bold response to the Caliph's remark about their marriage highlighted the delicate balance of power between the Abbasids and their powerful subjects.

During the reign of al-Mu'tadid's son, al-Muktafi, Tulunid Egypt was reabsorbed into the Abbasid Caliphate. Elsewhere, however, Abbasid control continued to erode. In Arabia, the Qarmatians, a Shi'ite faction, attacked pilgrims en route to Mecca and even stole the Black Stone from the Ka'ba, a severe blow to Abbasid prestige.

In Central Asia, the Persian Samanids declared independence and established their own empire. This marked the Persian Intermezzo, a period when native Persian dynasties ruled over Persia once again. The Abbasid caliph, increasingly a symbolic figure, lost control of the administration and military and handed over to the amir al-umara, or commander of the commanders.

The Buyids, Shi'ite warlords from northwestern Persia, eventually seized control of Iraq and Persia and triumphantly entered Baghdad. The Sunni Abbasid caliphs retained their titles but were reduced to figureheads under Buyid dominance.

Around the same time, the Fatimids, another Shi'ite dynasty, conquered Egypt and founded Cairo as the capital of their own caliphate. This era, sometimes called the 'Shi'ite century,' saw Shi'ite dynasties dominate much of the Muslim world. However, this dominance was soon challenged by a new Sunni power—the Seljuk Turks—emerging from Central Asia.

Chapter Five

The Seljuk Empire (1037–1194 CE)

Origins and Expansion

The Rise of the Seljuk Turks and Their Expansion into the Islamic World

The nomadic groups of warriors that established themselves in new areas were the first to emerge to prominence as the Turks. The war and split among Sunni and Shi'ite Muslims was causing the Islamic Empire to wane by the ninth century. Consequently, various empires started to emerge, and numerous regions developed their own identities.

Central Asian nomadic warriors, the Seljuk Turks progressively moved into Arab and northern Persian land. They were outstanding fighters who were proficient with bows and horses. As a pioneer tribe that embraced Islam, they won the confidence of the local populace. They served in Arab and Persian armies and offered protection to burgeoning empires. The Turks eventually conquered other areas as their strength grew.

Rooted in the rich tapestry of Turkic nomadic traditions and Islamic civilisation, the Seljuk Empire emerged as a pivotal force in the medieval Islamic world. This ascent occurred against a backdrop of fragmentation within the Islamic world and the encroaching influence of the Byzantine Empire. The decline of the Abbasid Caliphate, internal strife in the Byzantine Empire, and shifting power dynamics in Central Asia created a complex geopolitical landscape that set the stage for the Seljuk Turks' rise.

Led by Seljuk Beg, a visionary chieftain, the Seljuks united disparate Turkic tribes through military prowess and diplomatic acumen. This cohesion laid the foundation for a powerful confederation that bore his name. By the mid-11th century, the Seljuks had reached the threshold of the Islamic world, encountering the fragmented remnants of the Abbasid Caliphate and diminished local dynasties.

Key Military Campaigns and Territorial Acquisitions

The Seljuks seized the opportunity presented by the political vacuum, embarking on a series of military campaigns that propelled them to regional prominence. These conquests were marked by strategic acumen, opportunistic alliances, and military might. Charismatic leaders like Tughril Beg and Alp Arslan led their forces in decisive campaigns that reshaped the region's power dynamics.

One pivotal moment in Seljuk expansion was the Battle of Dandanqan in 1040, when Alp Arslan decisively defeated the Ghaznavid Sultanate. This victory solidified the Seljuks' control over Persia and laid the groundwork for future conquests. Buoyed by their military successes, the Seljuks continued their westward advance, bringing vast territories under their control and asserting dominance over rival powers.

A defining achievement of the Seljuk conquests was the capture of Baghdad in 1055, where Tughril Beg entered the city as a liberator. Recognised as the de facto ruler of the Abbasid Caliphate, Tughril's triumph symbolised the Seljuks' role as protectors of Sunni Islam and guardians of the Abbasid legacy.

Beyond military conquests, the Seljuks employed strategic alliances and diplomatic manoeuvres to consolidate their power. Through marriage alliances and agreements with local leaders, they secured the loyalty of diverse cultures and ethnicities within the Islamic world.

The culmination of Seljuk power was the establishment of the Seljuk Sultanate, a centralised state led by Malik Shah. This period marked the zenith of Seljuk influence, encompassing territories from Anatolia to Central Asia. Malik Shah's reign was distinguished by cultural and intellectual flourishing, with the Seljuk court becoming a hub of artistic and scholarly activity.

The Seljuks' ascent and territorial expansion were not merely about military conquests but also about fostering a legacy of governance and cultural prosperity. Their rise reshaped the medieval Islamic world, leaving an enduring historical mark.

Governance and Cultural Contributions

The Seljuk Administrative System and Contributions to Islamic Culture

One of the most significant battles in Seljuk history was the Battle of Manzikert, in which Alp Arslan decisively defeated the Byzantine Empire. This victory paved the way for Seljuk expansion into Anatolia. The capture of Baghdad was another pivotal moment, solidifying Seljuk control over the Abbasid Caliphate and establishing the Seljuks as a preeminent power in the Islamic world.

Throughout history, the Seljuks waged successful military campaigns against rival powers such as the Fatimids, the Ghaznavids, and the Crusader States. The conquest of Jerusalem by Seljuk forces under Malik Shah marked a high point of Seljuk military achievement, demonstrating their ability to project power beyond the confines of their empire.

In addition to battlefield conquests, the Seljuks employed diplomatic and economic strategies to expand their influence and secure their borders. They forged alliances with neighbouring powers, negotiated treaties, and engaged in trade diplomacy to strengthen their position and extend their reach across the Islamic world.

The Seljuk Empire fostered a vibrant cultural and artistic milieu, synthesising Turkic, Persian, and Islamic influences. Under their rule, arts and architecture flourished, with Sultans and elite patrons commissioning magnificent mosques, palaces, and public works that adorned their urban landscapes.

Seljuk architecture is renowned for its distinctive blend of Islamic geometric motifs, Persian decorative elements, and Turkic architectural forms. The Great Mosque of Isfahan, constructed during the reign of Malik Shah, stands as a masterpiece, featuring intricate tilework, soaring minarets, and elaborately carved mihrabs. Other notable examples of Seljuk architecture include the Alaeddin Mosque in Konya, the Masjid-e Jame in Isfahan, and the Sultanhan Caravanserai along the Silk Road.

Patronage of Art, Architecture, and Education

Beyond mosques and palaces, the Seljuks also patronised the construction of madrasas, libraries, and public baths. These architectural marvels served as centres of learning, community gathering, and spiritual contemplation. They reflected the grandeur and sophistication of the Seljuk civilisation and facilitated the exchange of ideas, knowledge, and cultural expression across diverse communities.

The Seljuk Empire became a bastion of intellectual inquiry and scholarly pursuit, attracting scholars, poets, and theologians from across the Islamic world.

Scholarship flourished under Seljuk patronage, with figures such as Omar Khayyam, Ibn Sina, and al-Ghazali making significant contributions to mathematics, medicine, philosophy, and theology. Omar Khayyam's treatises on algebra and astronomy, Ibn Sina's "Canon of Medicine," and al-Ghazali's works on Islamic theology and mysticism exemplify the breadth of Seljuk intellectual achievement.

Madrasas played a central role in Seljuk education, providing students with instruction in Islamic law, theology, Arabic grammar, and the sciences. Scholars and students gathered to study classical texts, engage in debates, and participate in intellectual exchanges that enriched the empire's landscape.

The Seljuk Empire was characterised by religious pluralism and tolerance, as Muslims, Christians, Jews, and other religious communities coexisted within its diverse society. While Islam was the state's dominant religion, the Seljuks adopted a policy of pluralism that granted freedom of worship and protected the rights of religious minorities. Mosques, synagogues, and churches flourished, reflecting the diverse religious traditions of the empire's inhabitants.

The Seljuks respected the religious rights and customs of non-Muslim communities, allowing them to practice their faiths freely and participate in communal life without fear of persecution. They also encouraged interfaith dialogue and cooperation, as scholars and theologians from different traditions engaged in debates and intellectual exchanges, fostering mutual understanding. The Seljuks facilitated the translation of classical texts from Greek, Persian, and Sanskrit into Arabic, promoting the dissemination of knowledge across linguistic and cultural boundaries.

The Seljuk Empire was a pivotal player in the diplomatic and commercial networks of the medieval Islamic world. Through diplomacy and trade, the Seljuks forged alliances, negotiated treaties, and facilitated the flow of goods, ideas, and cultural exchange across regional boundaries. Diplomacy was central to Seljuk's foreign policy, with marriage alliances, tribute payments, and military coalitions securing borders, maintaining stability, and expanding influence.

Trade flourished under Seljuk rule. The city's strategic location at the crossroads of trade routes connecting Europe, Asia, and Africa facilitated the exchange of goods, commodities, and cultural artefacts.

Cities like Baghdad, Isfahan, and Aleppo emerged as vibrant commercial hubs where merchants and artisans converged for commerce and cultural exchange. The Silk Road played a crucial role, with caravans carrying silk, spices, and precious metals traversing Seljuk territories to distant markets. Taxes on trade caravans and regulated commercial activities contributed to the empire's economic prosperity and fiscal stability.

The Seljuk Empire left a profound legacy, influencing Byzantine territories, Crusader States, and the broader Islamic world. Their military, diplomatic, cultural, and intellectual achievements continue to be a testament to their enduring impact on medieval history.

Chapter Six

The Fatimid Caliphate (909–1171 CE)

Founding and Establishment

The first Shia dynasty, the Fatimid Caliphate, ruled over Egypt and North Africa for over two and a half centuries, from 909 to 1171 AD. They were believed to be the true heirs of Hazrat Muhammad's (PBUH) daughter, Hazrat Fatima (RA), hence their name, Fatimid.

With a spirit of tolerance, the Fatimids ruled over a variety of areas with diverse religious traditions. Their rule was characterised by meritocracy, diversity, and pluralism. The Fatimid era was significant and distinctive both then and now because of the cultural and educational accomplishments made possible by their efficient government.

The Origins of the Fatimid Caliphate and its Establishment in North Africa

The Fatimid period (909–1171), which spanned from North Africa to Palestine and was governed by the Ismaili Fatimid caliphs, is considered a glorious period in history. To maintain and fortify their authority, the first three Fatimid caliphs had to overcome numerous obstacles.

For instance, the founder, Caliph al-Mahdi, had to deal with internal and external uprisings, such as Abu Abd Allah al-Shii and the Abu Yazid revolt, which nearly destroyed the new dynasty. Under Caliph al-Muizz's leadership, the regime was stable, with both internal stability and exterior growth.

Research, literature, institutional growth, and cultural improvements peaked during this period. The Fatimids promoted various fields of science, commerce, and culture, created efficient administrative and financial structures, and focused particularly on the study of Islam. Cairo, the capital of the Fatimids, developed into a global Islamic conurbation.

The true Islamic spirit of plurality, diversity, and tolerance blossomed during this period. Al-Qadi al-Nauman (d. 363–975) codified Ismaili law, and Ismaili literature was also at its height. Education and research were highly valued, which fostered an ethic of empathy and sharing, a spirit of inquiry, strict government, and respect for other societies.

Religious and Cultural Influence

Promoting tolerance, particularly towards non-Muslim minorities and other communities of Islam that adhered to differing schools of thought, was one of the distinctive characteristics of the Fatimid Dynasty. The Fatimids were exceedingly respectful and understanding of the faiths of the people they controlled despite adhering to the Shia Ismaili School of philosophy and legislation.

This was evident during the invasion of Egypt in 969, when Jawhar as-Siqili, the Fatimid army commander, offered the Egyptian people aman (an assurance of protection) on behalf of the Fatimid Caliph ai-Muizz in exchange for their acceptance and approval of Fatimid rule. The aman emphasised:

- Individuals from various religions were permitted to congregate in their places of worship and carry out their rituals.

- The foundation of all Islamic responsibilities was the Quran and the Prophet's (PBUH) Sunnah.

- The previous custom was adhered to for the treatment of the Dhimmis.

The Fatimids upheld the promises made in their renowned aman to ensure public safety. All groups, including Sunni Muslims, were granted religious freedom, and they never compelled their people to convert to Shiism, the official state religion. Their missionary call (Ismaili Da'wa), which encouraged people to think about and adhere to the Ismaili faith, led to the founding of the Fatimid dynasty in North Africa (909) and later in Egypt (969).

Studying Ismaili ideas and the faith's esoteric and exoteric understanding were encouraged by the da'wa. Ismaili Da'is (Missionaries) spread it by presenting the faith both individually and collectively through wisdom sessions, also known as Majalis al-Hikma.

Peace, tranquillity, and respect between many nations and religions were observed throughout Egypt's Fatimid dynasty. The cultural and social ties between the various communities were harmonious.

The Geniza manuscripts of Cairo, produced by the Jewish population between the eleventh and thirteenth centuries, are the primary sources of the economic and social development of the Fatimid and Ayyubid dynasties. They designate a wide range of court cases, business dealings, private letters, accounts, and marriage and divorce procedures.

This is how the Fatimid monarchs established a broad legal framework that allowed various communities to freely perform their religious duties, celebrations, and customs while enforcing market regulations in conformity with the Sunnah and Quran.

Treatment with a Diverse Populace

In 909, the Fatimids took control of North Africa, and in 969, they extended their rule to Egypt. Both regions at the time were home to a multi-religious and multiethnic population. Freedom of opinion and faith allowed each of these groups to carry out their own customs and ceremonies. "You shall continue in your madhab, and you shall be permitted to fulfil your obligations in accordance with religious scholarship," the aman stated. All communities were permitted to carry out religious rituals and ceremonies during Caliph al-Aziz's rule.

The Fatimids enjoyed constructing large areas like al-Azhar and al-Anwar, as well as mosques. They also rebuilt Christian churches, erected such places for Sunni Muslims, and provided funding for the upkeep of their places of worship. According to Christian writer Mawhub B. Masur, churches enjoyed tranquillity and safety throughout the reigns of Caliphs al Muizz and al-Aziz, and the celebration and practice of religious ceremonies became one of the key characteristics of his government. Another distinctive aspect of this dynasty was meritocracy. There are several instances of people with brains, talent, vision, and inventiveness being appointed to the highest positions without regard to their race, faith, country, or religion.

The initial vizier of the Fatimid dynasty was Abu al-Faraj Yaqub bin Killis (d. 99 CE), a Jewish man who converted to Islam. Quzman b. Mina, a Christian, was appointed as a member of the chief advisors' team in the financial area throughout the reign of Caliph al-Aziz. He later served as an officer in the Kharaj bureau in Egypt.

Abul-Fath Mansur b. Muqashir, a Christian physician, was also Caliph Al-Aziz's personal physician. Bahram, a Christian vazir under Caliph al-Hafiz (1130–49), was given titles such as Sayf-al-Islam, Taj-al-Dawla, and Taj-al-Muluk, which had never before been given to a non-Muslim.

Abu Saad alTustari, a Jew, headed Caliph al-Mustansir's mother's office. The Fatimid judicial system included many Sunni judges, as well as Christians and Jews. Caliph al-Mansur appointed a Maliki administrator.

Instead of appointing an Ismaili or Shia judge, Muhammad b.Abi☐lM anzur chose Qayarwan. This practice was applied in other Fatimid areas, where Sunni qadis were appointed to govern cities predominantly inhabited by a Sunni majority. Caliph al Muizz had an equally skilled Qadi Numan by his side, but he nevertheless named Qadi Abu Tahir as the Chief Judge of Egypt when he arrived and took power. This was in contrast to the Ikshi did administration's Chief Justice Abu Tahir.

> *The Holy Quran says: "O mankind, indeed we have created you from male and female and made you peoples and tribes that you may know one another indeed the most noble of you in the sight of Allah is the most righteous of you Indeed, Allah knows and acquainted." (Quran, 49:13)*

The Quran best explains the idea of diversity and pluralism in Islam. Islam is tolerant of cultural and religious diversity and opposes demeaning or mocking the identity of others. In fact, it exhorts Muslims to assist people from all walks of life. The numerous nations of many ethnic and religious groupings were part of the Fatimid masses.

Through their effective leadership, their monarchs established wholesome, beneficial environments that allowed people to coexist peacefully and harmoniously. The Fatimids fostered an environment for learning and the development of cultural and commercial endeavours by collaborating with various groups under the tenets of diversity and pluralism. For this reason, the Fatimid era was characterised by pluralism.

Principles of Good Governance Observed

The Islamic values that Prophet Muhammad (PBUH) taught and upheld were similar to the Fatimid governmental ideals of social justice and equality. The Fatimids were a minority in the Fatimid polity, which Sunnis and Kharjis in North Africa dominated, just like Muslims were in the city of Medina. The principles of inclusion and just governance were the foundation for the Medina Charter, which the Prophet drafted. In a similar vein, the aman sent into Egypt by the Fatimid commander Jawhar for the benefit of the Fatimid Caliph al-Muizz showed acceptance and tranquillity.

The following was emphasised and ensured in the Aman document:

- Affirmation of the Fatimid Imam-Caliphs' authority
- Commitment to fair governance for all
- Recognition of the Fatimid Caliph-Imam's responsibility to address the needs of the people
- Assurance of life and property protection for the general population
- Promotion of the social welfare of the public
- Presentation of a framework of laws to guide and regulate governance.

It was the Fatimid monarchs who fulfilled the promises made in the aman text. Additionally, they established agencies that exemplified best practices for the efficient operation of the state. They hired former officials from the previous administrations for their diwans without hesitation. Many departments were shut down for efficient administration, and new diwans, such as Diwan al-Kashf, were established.

The Spirit of Inquiry: Knowledge was patronised by the Caliphs of the Fatimids. They believed that information should be shared rather than kept to oneself. To encourage the development and exchange of knowledge, they founded libraries as well as educational, academic, and research institutes.

During the Fatimid era, Cairo developed into a hub for learning, drawing intellectuals and information seekers from around the globe. Following the takeover of Egypt, General Jawhar established the first mosque, known as "Jami-al-Azhar," and al-Qahira al-Muizziayya (the triumphant one of the al-Muizz), under the guidance and teaching of Caliph al-Muziz, who was then in North Africa. By 378/984, al-Azhar had developed into a university with both male and female classes.

Dar al-Ilm: Dar al-Ilm (House of Knowledge), founded in 395/1005 by Caliph al-Hakim, was another important educational establishment founded by the Fatimids. Like in contemporary universities today, a wide range of subjects were taught there.

A vast array of subjects, including mathematics, astronomy, lexicology, medicine, religion, and many more, were chosen to be studied simultaneously by the students. Additionally, it served as a training centre for Ismaili dais, who participated in Ismaili dawa both inside and outside of Cairo. The opening and operation of Dar al-Ilm are described in detail by al-Musabbhi, the renowned court biographer of the Fatimid Caliph al-Hakim.

The structure had nice furnishings:

- Professionals from every field were employed and paid fairly.
- Free paper, ink, and reeds were given to visitors at Dar al-Ilm.
- Visitors and students from all walks of life came here to study.
- Scholars greatly benefited from the Caliph al-Hakim's personal number of books on many subjects, which were donated to Dar al-Ilm.

The lecturers at Dar al-Ilm received salaries similar to those at al-Azhar. The waqaf, which al-Hakim founded for the upkeep of the Rashida, al-Azhar, and Dar al-Ilm mosques, provided additional funding for the organisation. The well-known Mumluk historian al-Maqrizi has also described the various purchases made with this money. Among the many accomplishments of al-Hakim's Dar al-Ilm was the creation of the astrological chart Zij-al-Hakimi by al-Yunus, who did it without the use of an observatory. The astronomers of al-Mamun in the astrological observatory at Shamasiya prepared the previous Zij, which this one replaced.

At Daral-Ilm, Ibn al-Haytham worked for the Caliph/Imam al-Hakim. He was a successful scientist whose contributions have earned him the title of "Father of Modern Optics." In the realm of optics, his book Kitab al-Manazrat is a significant contribution. It is significant to remember that every chief dais in charge of Ismaili missions across various Jazeeras studied various subjects in Dar al-Ilm for a while.

It is clear that a variety of subjects were taught at this institution. Caliph al-Hakim himself developed the goals and regulations of Dar al-Ilm and oversaw its direct management. During the Fatimid era, numerous official and unofficial educational institutions promoted a spirit of inquiry among the populace and helped with educational progress.

Cultural Development: Additionally, the Fatimids supported the arts and culture. They built cities such as Mahdiya, Khalisa, and Mansuria since they established their authority in North Africa in 909. When the Fatimids overran Egypt in 969 and established the new capital of al-Qahira al-Muizziyya (The triumphant One of al-Muizz), their art and architecture achieved their pinnacle. The two palaces in this carefully designed new Fatimid capital city—one for the Caliph and one for his successor—were set apart by a sizable space known as Bayn al Qasrayn that was used for public meetings and rituals.

In Cairo, the gates of Babul FatuhandBab Zuwayla were added, and a magnificent mosque known as al-Azhar (the Radiant) was constructed. The city had palaces, mosques, libraries, and educational institutions.

In addition to architecture, ornamental arts were frequently employed in a variety of media, including fabrics, glass, crystal, stone, stucco, and wood carving.

Dinar and Dharam, two Fatimid coins, were renowned for their style and purity and considered elegantly constructed. Their coins reflected the artistic preferences and beliefs of the Fatimids. Because of their exceptional quality and quantity, these coins became the most extensively used throughout Egypt and the surrounding area. Instead of creating their own currency when the Crusaders took over Palestine, they imitated the modern Fatimid coins.

Eyewitness reports of cultural evolution by al-Musabhi, Maqrizi, and Nasir Khusraw situate Egypt in a unique position both inside and outside the Islamic world. During the Fatimid era, it developed into a major manufacturing hub. In Fatimid Egypt, a wide variety of craftspeople were employed. Compared to ancient Rome, the quantity of artisans was superior.

Badr and his successors delayed the fall of the Fatimid state for almost a century, preventing its collapse. In response to the eastern Seljuq assault, Badr employed both religious and secular weaponry to conduct an active agenda in Syria, Arabia, and other places. Despite these efforts, the Fatimid troops were repeatedly routed in Syria, and their fan base in Arabia was diminished to negligible proportions.

Al-Afḍal, Badr's son and heir, effectively gave up the Egyptian Fatimid dynasty's claims to the worldwide caliphate. Following the death of al-Mustanṣir in 1094, al-Affal played a pivotal role in the defeat of the succession. Although al-Mustanṣir had proposed his older son, Nizar, as his successor with the approval of Isma'ili chiefs, al-Afdal favoured Aḥmad, the younger son. Ahmad was a young man without friends and would be totally reliant on his sponsor. To secure his influence, al-Afḍal married his sister to Aḥmad and declared him caliph under the regnal title al-Mustaʿli (reigned 1094–1101), thereby dividing the group from top to bottom.

This decision sparked some dissent, even within Egypt. Under the leadership of Ḥasan-e Ṣabbaḥ, the Isma'ili mission in Persia, Iraq, and Central Asia severed ties with the Fatimid rulers in Cairo. Refusing to acknowledge the new caliph, this group, known as the Nizari Isma'iliyyah (referred to as the Assassins by its critics) declared Nizar and his successors as the legitimate imams while denouncing the caliphs in Cairo as usurpers.

When al-Musta'li's son al-Amir (reigned 1101–30) was killed by the Nizari Assassins, his cousin al-Ḥafiẓ (reigned 1130–49) succeeded him. However, this transition caused further fragmentation. Isma'ili, primarily in Yemen, who had previously accepted al-Musta'li, broke away in 1130. According to the Yemenis, al-Ḥafiẓ and his successors were not recognised since al-Amir had left an infant son who was now the concealed imam.

By 1171, the dynasty came to an end. Without authority, sway, or hope, the final four caliphs were merely a local Egyptian dynasty. The final caliph passed away in 1171. The Fatimid caliphate, which was already extinct as a political and religious entity, was officially abolished, and Saladin, the vizier in name, assumed the role of the true ruler of Egypt.

Chapter Seven

The Mamluk Sultanate (1250–1517 CE)

Origins and Rise to Power

From the middle of the 13th century to the beginning of the 16th century, Egypt, the Levant, and the Hejaz were governed by the Mamluk Sultanate, also called Mamluk Egypt or the Mamluk Empire. A sultan oversaw a military caste of mamluks, or emancipated slave soldiers, who governed it. The Ayyubid dynasty was overthrown in Egypt in 1250, establishing the sultanate, which the Ottoman Empire overthrew in 1517.

Based on the major ethnicity or corps of the reigning Mamluks during these respective eras, Mamluk history is often divided into two periods: the Circassian or Burji period (1382–1517) and the Turkic or Bahri period (1250–1382).

After usurping power from his successor in 1250, the first sultanate rulers were members of the Mamluk troops of the Ayyubid sultan as-Salih Ayyub (r. 1240–1249). The Mongols' southerly progress was stopped in 1260 when the Mamluks, led by Baybars and Sultan Qutuz, overran them. They then took control of the Syrian principalities ruled by the Ayyubids or established suzerainty over them.

By the end of the 13th century, they had overrun the Crusader nations and spread into southern Anatolia, Makuria (Nubia), Cyrenaica, and the Hejaz thanks to the efforts of sultans Baybars, Qalawun (r. 1279–1290), and al-Ashraf Khalil (r. 1290–1293). The third tenure of al-Nasir Muhammad (r. 1293–1294, 1299–1309, 1310–1341) saw a prolonged era of calm and prosperity for the sultanate before the internal conflict that marked his sons' succession when senior emirs retained the real power.

One such emir, Barquq, established Burji power by toppling the sultan twice in 1382 and 1390. Under his successors, Mamluk power throughout the empire declined due to natural calamities, tribal uprisings, and foreign invasions, and the Empire experienced a protracted period of financial hardship. Sultan Barsbay made significant attempts to restock the coffers, primarily through tax excursions into the countryside and the monopolisation of trade with Europe.

Key Battles and Achievements in Establishing Mamluk Rule

Mamluks and Mongols: By driving the Mongol invaders from the area, the Mamluk Dynasty preserved Islam in Egypt and guaranteed Egypt's continued Muslim status. The Mamluks overcame the Mongols at the pivotal Battle of Ayn Jalut, which took place in what is now Israel, not far from Nazareth.

This victory prevented the Mongols from controlling Egypt and forcing their ideas on the Muslim populace. The forces of General Baybars' Mamluk Bahri Sultan al-Muzaffar Sayf al-Din Qutuz and Mongolian General Ked-Buqa, who fought for Khan Hulago, the Mongolian ruler of Iran, engaged in combat in September 1260 CE.

King David, who was then a young Israelite boy and would go on to become a key figure in the Judeo-Christian belief tradition, was thought to have fought the giant Goliath at Ayn Jalut and won a significant victory for King Saul along with his army over the Philistines.

With an estimated 20,000 warriors on each side, the chances were more evenly distributed in the conflict between the Mamluks and the Mongols than they were for King David. Despite having armies of equal size, the Mamluks' shrewd tactics and a general who knew the terrain ultimately gave them the upper hand, which stopped the Mongols' westward advance.

Mamluks and Crusaders: The Mamluk Dynasty played a key role in ending the Crusades by engaging in numerous conflicts with the Crusaders. In 1291 CE, Bahri Sultan al-Ashraf Khalil was able to retake Acre from the Crusaders. Located in what is now northern Israel, Acre was a strategically significant port city on the Mediterranean. It would have been a prize for any army and essential for transportation, trade, and commerce. There was a huge carnage once the Mamluks took control of the city. The Knights Templar was the last to resist the Mamluks, but they eventually took control of the city's area, where they had their headquarters for more than a century.

Many Templar Knights were put to death after the city fell, but some escaped and were able to relocate their headquarters to Arwad Island. The Crusades ended in 1303 CE when the Mamluk Dynasty defeated the Templars once more in the Siege of Arwad. The Crusaders lost their last stronghold in the Holy Land when the island was destroyed, and as a result, Christianity's military presence virtually disappeared.

Authority over Medina and Mecca: Throughout the later middle Ages, the holy cities of Mecca and Medina were part of the Mamluks' biggest Islamic kingdom.

Governance and Prosperity

For nearly three centuries, the Mamluk Sultanate in Egypt was one of the major powers in the world. More importantly, mamlukism's institutional frameworks were widespread throughout the Muslim world and continued in one form or another for almost a thousand years.

Property Rights Regimes and Economic Growth

What is meant by property rights, and does the concept of private property extend into the past? The phrase "property right" in the current economics literature refers to an owner's ability to utilise an item or good for income generation or consumption, transfer that asset to another party, and enter into agreements with third parties to rent, pledge, or mortgage that asset or good. Prevalent property rights regimes assist people in establishing expectations regarding their economic contacts with others since they address fundamental concerns related to financial interactions.

Political economists contend that insecure property rights cause a variety of detrimental externalities, such as slowed rental and collateral markets, expropriation risk-induced investment distortions, and expenses related to defending insecure property. According to Acemoglu, Johnson, and Robinson, the governing bodies of private property are necessary to promote strong economic performance. In contrast to the "limited access order" that legal and political systems use to safeguard claims on private property, the "natural state" that North, Wallis and Weingast define is autocratic and nepotistic.

So far as it emphasises the value of private property rights in promoting economic growth, the body of existing literature is persuasive. However, little is known about the factors that influence private property rights regimes globally throughout time. There is extensive documentation of the development of rights to private property in Europe, especially in England. According to North and Thomas, elites' attempts to take advantage of landowners' rents led to the development of English land laws in the thirteenth century.

The resulting property rights system was effective because it discouraged rent-seeking and excessive taxation while incentivising people to create and innovate. According to North, promoting strong forms of economic development required both contracting institutions and property rights. According to Acemoglu and Johnson's empirical analysis of the significance of property rights in relation to contracting institutions, property rights are a reliable indicator of financial development, investment, and economic progress.

During the middle Ages, Egypt and Syria were essential transit countries for global trade. The Mamluks increased the empire's involvement in international trade early in their reign. Baybars and Qalawun negotiated commercial treaties with Genoa and Ceylon, respectively. By the 15th century, the sultanate was in financial trouble due to internal Mamluk power battles, declining iqta' revenue from epidemics, and Bedouin tribes encroaching on abandoned farmlands.

The Mamluks used a three-pronged strategy to make up for these losses: taxing the middle classes in the cities, increasing the production and export of sugar and cotton to Europe, and making money off of their position as a transit country in the trade among Europe as well as the Far East. The Mamluks achieved their most profitable policy by strengthening trading relations with Venice, Genoa, and Barcelona and raising commodity tariffs. The Mamluks taxed the traders who operated or passed through the empire's ports during this period, and the long-standing trade between Europe and the Islamic world started to contribute significantly to state coffers.

Mamluk Egypt supplied raw materials to Western Europe and was a significant textile producer. While Europeans were producing more textiles, silk products, sugar, glass, soaps, and paper, the output of these items declined due to the numerous outbreaks of the Black Plague. Nevertheless, during the Crusades, trade with the Muslims persisted in defiance of papal prohibitions. Spices like pepper, muscat blossoms, nuts, cloves, and cinnamon, together with indigo and pharmaceuticals, dominated the Mediterranean trade.

Under Barsbay, a state monopoly on luxury commodities, specifically spices, was created. The state-regulated prices and kept a portion of the sales. Instead of using the imperial treasury, which was connected to the military's iqta' system, Barsbay took direct control of Alexandria, the main Egyptian commercial port, in 1387 and transferred its tax earnings to his personal treasury.

In 1429, he mandated that the spice trade with Europe be routed via Cairo before commodities arrived in Alexandria to prevent the direct movement of spices from the Red Sea to Alexandria. The Mamluk-Venetian monopoly on trans-Mediterranean trade saw a sharp decline in revenue in the late 15th and early 16th centuries due to Portuguese expansion into Africa and Asia, which accompanied and contributed to the sultanate's downfall.

Internal Challenges and External Threats Leading to the Decline of the Mamluk Sultanate

Egypt and Syria returned to being provinces within an empire after the Ottomans defeated the Mamluks in 1516–1517. Despite the fall of the Mamluk sultanate, the Mamluks continued to be a dominant class in Egypt and held significant political power. Slave market purchases continued to resupply the Mamluk elite, as they had done under the Mamluk dynasty. Following a period of apprenticeship, slaves continued to make up the majority of the army and were soon being assigned to positions inside the Ottoman government. Thus, the Mamluks were able to gradually penetrate and eventually take control of the Ottoman ruling class.

One significant invention altered the Mamluks' personality. Sons of Mamluks were previously prohibited from participating in any regiment other than non-slave ones and from holding positions in the state that were designated for Mamluks during the Mamluk sultanate. However, the sons were no longer denied these benefits during Ottoman control, which caused kinship ties to erode the Mamluk values of loyalty and unity.

The Ottoman administrators could maintain some influence over Egyptian politics to the extent that they could capitalise on the Mamluk division. However, the Mamluks once again had essentially complete authority over the army, the government, and the revenue by the end of the 17th century, when Ottoman influence was waning across the empire. Istanbul was eventually relegated to acknowledging the independence of the Mamluk group, which would ensure the Ottomans received a specific amount each year. As a result, Napoleon faced Mamluk forces and a Mamluk state when he invaded Egypt in 1798 in a massacre in 1811; Egypt's new ruler, Muḥammad Alī Pasha, ultimately shattered their dominance there.

Chapter Eight

The Ottoman Empire (1299-1922 CE)

Foundation and Expansion

Among the strongest and most enduring dynasties in history was the Ottoman Empire. For about 600 years, a sizable portion of the Middle East, Eastern Europe, and North Africa were governed by this Islamic superpower. Over his subjects, the Sultan, the chief leader, was granted total religious and political power. Although they were largely seen as a threat by Western Europeans, many historians consider the Ottoman Empire to have contributed significantly to regional peace and security as well as significant advancements in art, science, religion, and culture.

The Founding of the Ottoman Empire and Early Expansion under Osman I and His Successors

Osman I, a Turkoman tribal leader, established a beylik, or territory, in northwest Anatolia around 1299, laying the groundwork for what would become a vast empire. By the middle of the fourteenth century, his successors had turned this little kingdom into a transcontinental empire, conquering much of Anatolia and spreading into the Balkans. With Mehmed II's capture of Constantinople in 1453, the Ottomans brought an end to the Byzantine Empire and became a significant regional force. Under Suleiman the Magnificent (1520–1566) rule, the empire reached its zenith in terms of political development, wealth, and power.

At the beginning of the 17th century, the Ottomans ruled over 32 provinces and a large number of vassal kingdoms, which were either eventually absorbed into the empire or given varying degrees of autonomy. For six centuries, the Ottoman Empire dominated relations between the Middle East and Europe, with its capital at Constantinople (present-day Istanbul) and dominion over a sizable chunk of the Mediterranean Basin.

Although Suleiman the Magnificent's death was once believed to have signalled the beginning of the Ottoman Empire's decline, contemporary academic opinion holds that the empire maintained a robust and adaptable economy, society, and military throughout a large portion of the 18th century. The Ottoman military structure, however, lagged behind those of its main European competitors, the Habsburg and Russian empires, during the protracted peace that lasted from 1740 until 1768.

Due to devastating military setbacks in the late 18th and early 19th centuries, the Ottoman Empire suffered significant territorial losses and a decline in international prestige. This led to a thorough reform and modernisation process called the Tanzimat. Despite further territorial losses, particularly in the Balkans, where several new states arose, the Ottoman state became much more powerful and well-organised internally over the course of the 19th century.

The Young Turk Revolution of 1908, spearheaded by the Committee of Union and Progress (CUP), marked the beginning of the Second Constitutional Era and the introduction of competitive multi-party elections according to a constitutional monarchy. This was the culmination of Ottoman intellectuals' efforts to liberalise society and politics along European lines, beginning in the late 19th century. However, after the catastrophic Balkan Wars, the CUP grew more radical and patriotic, and in 1913, they led a coup d'etat that resulted in a one-party system.

In an attempt to break free from the diplomatic isolation that had led to its recent territorial losses, the CUP formed an alliance with the German Empire and sided with the Central Powers during World War I. The empire battled internal dissension, particularly the Arab Revolt, but was able to hold its own during the war for the most part. During this time, the Ottoman administration committed devastating genocide against Greeks, Armenians, and Assyrians.

The Ottoman Empire lost its southern lands to France and the United Kingdom when the victorious Allied Powers conquered and divided it following World War I. The Republic of Turkey emerged in the Anatolian heartland as a result of Mustafa Kemal Atatürk's successful Turkish War of Independence against the occupying Allies. The Ottoman Empire was officially ended in 1922 when the Ottoman monarchy was abolished.

Golden Age and Governance

Following his historic victory in the Battle of Mohács in 1526, Suleiman the Magnificent (1520–1566) established Ottoman rule in what is now Hungary and other Central European territories. He also captured Belgrade in 1521 and the southern and central regions of the Kingdom of Hungary during the Ottoman–Hungarian Wars.

In 1529, he besieged Vienna but was unable to capture the city. He attempted to invade Vienna once more in 1532 but was defeated during the siege of Güns. Wallachia, Transylvania, and occasionally Moldavia were made into vassal realms of the Empire. To obtain control of Mesopotamia and naval access to the Persian Gulf, the Ottoman Turks captured Baghdad from the Persians in 1535. The Caucasus was first divided between the Safavids as well as the Ottomans in 1555, and this division persisted until the conclusion of the Russo-Turkish War (1768–1774).

Following the Peace of Amasya, southern Dagestan, Armenia, Georgia, and Azerbaijan remained Persian, while the Ottomans took over western Armenia, western Kurdistan, and western Georgia. In 1539, a successful siege of the Spanish outpost of Castelnuovo on the Adriatic coast resulted in 8,000 Ottoman casualties. The following year, Venice agreed to terms and gave up the majority of its kingdom in the Aegean and the Morea. The Ottoman military force numbered 60,000 at this time.

Driven by mutual hostility toward Habsburg authority, France and the Ottoman Empire formed an alliance. Under the leadership of Ottoman admirals Hayreddin Barbarossa and Dragut, this corporation led the capture of Nice (1543) and Corsica (1553). These campaigns were the collaborative efforts orchestrated by Sultan Suleiman the Magnificent and the King Francis I of France.

During the Ottoman invasion of Esztergom in northern Hungary in 1543, France provided an artillery battalion to aid the Ottoman forces. In 1547, Ferdinand, the ruler of the Habsburgs, formally acknowledged Ottoman dominance in Hungary following additional Turkish advances. During the siege of Szigetvár in 1566, Suleiman passed away from natural causes. Several academics have disputed the notion that the Ottomans were waning after his death. At the end of Suleiman's rule, the Empire included three continents and covered over 877,888 square miles (2,273,720 km2).

In the late 14th century, the Ottoman Empire was initially organised into provinces, defined as geographical divisions with sultan-appointed governors. The Eyalet, also known as Pashalik or Beylerbeylik, was a Beylerbey's (or "lord of lords" or "governor") domain and was further divided into Sanjaks.

As part of the Tanzimat reforms, the "Vilayet Law" was enacted in 1864, bringing the Vilayets into being. The 1871 Vilayet Law added the nahiye to the hierarchy of administrative divisions created by the 1864 law, contrasting with the previous Eyalet structure.

Administrative Structure, Legal System and Contributions to Art and Culture

Before the 19th—and 20th-century reforms, the Ottoman Empire's state structure consisted of two primary components: the military and civil administrations. The Sultan was at the top of the hierarchy. Local administrative units based on regional features served as the foundation for civil administration.

The clergy were under state control. In Ottoman administrative circles, some pre-Islamic Turkish customs that had endured the adoption of Islamic Iranian legal and administrative procedures continued to hold significance. According to Ottoman thought, the state's primary duty was to protect and expand Muslim territory while maintaining peace and stability within its boundaries within the larger framework of dynastic sovereignty and orthodox Islamic practice.

For its size and duration, the Ottoman Empire—also known as the House of Osman as a dynastic institution—was unparalleled in the Islamic world. Only the House of Habsburg, which ruled from the late 13th to the early 20th centuries, had an equally uninterrupted line of sovereigns (kings/emperors) from the same family who held power for such a long time.

Because he was perceived as a threat to the empire, the reigning sultan was overthrown eleven times and replaced by another Ottoman dynasty ruler, typically a brother, son, or nephew. Only two unsuccessful attempts to overthrow the Ottoman dynasty throughout Ottoman history point to a political structure that could handle revolutions for a considerable amount of time without creating needless instability.

As a result, Mehmed VI (r. 1918–1922), the last Ottoman sultan, was a direct patrilineal (male-line) descendant of Osman I (d. 1323/4), which was unprecedented in the Islamic world and Europe (for example, the male line of the House of Habsburg went extinct in 1740). The main goal of the Imperial Harem was to guarantee the continuity of the Ottoman sultans' direct patrilineal (male-line) sovereignty in subsequent generations by ensuring the birth of male descendants to the Ottoman throne.

Beginning with Selim I, who founded the Ottoman Caliphate, the sultans claimed the highest status in Islam, that of caliph. Although he did not always have total authority, the Ottoman sultan, often known as the "lord of kings" or padişah, did not always wield absolute authority; he served as the sole regent of the empire and was seen as the personification of its governance.

A key institution of the Ottoman court was the Imperial Harem, overseen by the reigning sultan. While its primary purpose was domestic, the Harem's influence extended into state politics. During the period known as the "Sultanate of Women," the Harem's ladies essentially ran the government for a while.

The sons of the former sultan were always used to select new ones. The palace school's robust curriculum was designed to weed out unsuitable candidates for heirs and build support for a successor among the ruling class. No single course in the palace schools trained future state administrators. First, under Islamic custom, intellectuals and government officials were trained at the Madrasa (Medrese), which was reserved for Muslims.

Vakifs helped Medrese with its financial burden, enabling children from low-income households to advance in social standing and income. The second route was the Enderûn, a free boarding school for Christians that, through a process called Devshirme, enrolled 3,000 Christian boys between the ages of eight and twenty each year from one in forty households in the communities settled in Rumelia or the Balkans.

The sultan's political and executive power was delegated, notwithstanding his status as the ultimate monarch. To handle state politics, many ministers and advisors gathered around a council called diwan.

When the Ottoman Empire was still a Beylik, the diwan was made up of the tribe's elders.

Later, military officers and local elites (such as political and religious advisors) were added to the council's composition. In 1320, a Grand Vizier was established to take over some of the sultan's duties. The Grand Vizier's appointment, firing, and monitoring powers were nearly limitless, giving him significant autonomy from the sultan. Sultans stopped participating in politics in the late 16th century, and the Grand Vizier took over as the de facto head of state.

The Ottoman legal system recognised religious law's authority over its subjects. Sharia, or religious law, and Qanun, dynasty law, coexisted simultaneously. Local jurisprudence served as the foundation for the Ottoman Empire's organisational structure. Legal administration was a component of a broader plan to balance local and central authority. The administration of land rights, which allowed the local government to satisfy the demands of the local millet, was a major aspect of Ottoman power.

The Ottoman Empire's complicated jurisdiction system was designed to allow for the assimilation of diverse religious and cultural communities. Three court systems existed under the Ottoman Empire: the "trade court," a court for Muslims, and a court for non-Muslims, with appointed Jews and Christians in charge of each religious community. The administrative Qanun, or laws based on the Turkic Yassa and Töre and formed in the pre-Islamic period, governed the entire system.

However, these court types were not entirely exclusive. For example, the Islamic courts, which served as the Empire's main courts, could also resolve disputes between litigants of different religions or settle trade disputes. Jews and Christians frequently turned to these courts to get a more forceful ruling on a particular matter. Despite having the legal authority to do so through local governors, the Ottoman state chose to refrain from interfering in non-Muslim religious law systems.

The Quran, the Hadith, or sayings of Muhammad (PBUH), the ijma, or agreement of the Muslim community, the qiyas, or method of analogous reasoning from prior precedents, and regional customs were all combined to create the Islamic Sharia law system. The Empire's legal schools, located in Istanbul and Bursa, taught both systems.

Unlike conventional European courts, the Ottoman Islamic legal system was structured differently. A Qadi, or judge, presided over Islamic courts. Throughout the Ottoman Empire, Qadis have placed more emphasis on regional customs and traditions in the regions they oversaw than on legal precedent since the closure of the ijtihad, or "Gate of Interpretation." Due to the Ottoman court system's absence of an appeal framework, plaintiffs could use jurisdictional case techniques, moving their cases from one court system to another until they received a decision favouring them.

Significant changes were made to the Ottoman legal system in the late 19th century. The Gülhane Edict of 1839 marked the start of this legal modernisation movement. Among these reforms was the establishment of a system of "separate competences, religious and civil," the "fair and public trials of all accused regardless of religion," and the approval of testimony on non-Muslims. A code of civil procedure, civil codes (1869–1876), and specific land codes (1858) were also passed.

The implementation of a three-tiered court system indicates that these reforms were largely modelled after French models. With the final enactment of the Mecelle, a civil code that governed marriage, divorce, alimony, wills, and other aspects of personal status, this system—known as Nizamiye—was expanded to the level of local magistrates. An administrative council established that the Nizamiye courts were to address statutory matters, and the religious courts were to treat religious topics to make clear the separation of judicial powers.

Factors Leading to the Decline of the Ottoman Empire

Territorial Losses: Long before the Ottoman Empire completely fell apart, Ottoman territory started to break up. The 19th century saw the rise of independence movements. Greece, Romania, and Serbia were among the Ottoman territories that gained their independence. Other regions, like Bulgaria and Egypt under Muḥammad Ali, experienced a notable increase in autonomy. By the 20th century, more self-determination movements emerged, including Armenian, Arab, and Turkish nationalism, further challenging the unity of the empire.

Military Losses: In the Battle of Vienna in 1683 and the Battle of Lepanto in 1571, the Ottoman Empire's forces were routed.

Economic Challenges: When European nations started trading with East Asia and the East Indies by sea instead of via Ottoman-controlled land routes, the Ottoman Empire's economy suffered greatly. The empire's response to falling income, which included raising taxes and using confiscations, only made matters worse. By the middle of the 19th century, the empire had accumulated massive debt. In the 1870s, a worldwide financial crisis, drought, and flooding worsened the issue.

Corruption: Decadence and corruption weakened the empire's government.

Young Turk Revolution: The Young Turks conducted a revolt against Sultan Abdülhamid II's autocratic government, led by disgruntled military officers and college students. In 1908, the organisation successfully got Abdülhamid to reinstate the constitution from 1876. The following year, the sultan was overthrown by the Young Turks. The organisation fostered a fresh wave of Turkish nationalism after gaining power.

Reforms and Opposition: By implementing a number of reforms aimed at modernising the government, Ottoman sultans tried to save the empire. The Tanzimat reforms, which were implemented between

1839 and 1876, were the most significant of them. With the implementation of reforms in the fields of finance, management, justice, schooling, and the military, the Sultans consolidated their hold on power. However, when the Sultans gained control over all legal power, opposition developed, especially from a group of rebels known as the Young Turks.

World War I: At first, the Empire was not particularly concerned about how the war would turn out. For the most part, the Young Turk government favoured maintaining its neutrality. However, opportunists in the administration, like Enver Paşa, thought aiding Germany's war effort would revive the struggling empire, particularly when Germany appeared poised for victory in the early months of the conflict. But in the end, the Central Powers lost to the Allied powers. Ottoman territory was significantly diminished by the Treaty of Sèvres, the postwar agreement between the Ottomans and the Allies.

The Atatürk Rise: In Ankara, Turkey, a new administration led by Mustafa Kemal—later known as Atatürk—came into power. After the sultanate was abolished in 1922, Mehmed VI, the final Ottoman sultan, fled to Malta. Turkey was declared a republic in 1923. Its first president was Atatürk. This resulted in the expulsion of all Ottoman dynasty members from the nation.

Under Sultans Abdülmecid I and Abdülaziz's rule, the Ottoman Empire underwent a set of reforms known as Tanzimat (Turkish: "Reorganisation") between 1839 and 1876. These reforms, greatly influenced by European thought, aimed to transform the empire from its previous theocratic structure into a modern state.

The Hatt-I Şerif of Gülhane (1839; "Noble Edict of the Rose Chamber") outlined several of the Tanzimat reforms' main principles. Regardless of race or religion, this declaration called for creating new structures that would ensure the security of life, wealth, and honour for all subjects of the empire.

Additionally, it introduced more equitable systems of military conscription and educational opportunities and permitted the creation of a standardised tax system to eradicate abuses. Although the promises of equal treatment for non-Muslims residing in the empire were not always fulfilled, Mustafa Reşid Paşa, who held the position of grand vizier for six terms, was primarily responsible for implementing the remaining reforms outlined in the Noble Edict.

A new secular school system was established, the army was restructured according to the Prussian conscript system, provincial representative assemblies were established, and new criminal and commercial laws were introduced, many of which were based on French models. Furthermore, these rules were enforced by recently formed state courts not controlled by the Islamic religious council or ulama.

By the middle of the 1870s, during the latter years of Abdülaziz's rule, the Tanzimat reform movement had ended—the Tanzimat's attempt to consolidate power concentrated all legal authority in the sultan's hands. As a result, when Abdülaziz started abusing his position of authority and implementing revisionist policies, not much could be done. Despite this, the Tanzimat reforms successfully created the framework for the Ottoman state's slow modernisation.

Chapter Nine

The Mughal Empire (1526–1857 CE)

Establishment and Expansion

Two countries with a Muslim majority are located on the fringes of the Indian subcontinent: Pakistan on the west and Bangladesh on the east. Both of these countries, as well as the vast minority of Muslims living in India, have one dynasty to thank for their Muslim faith: the Mughal Dynasty.

The Rise of the Mughal Empire under Babur and its Expansion across the Indian Subcontinent

South Asia's first modern empire was the Mughal Empire. At its height, the empire spanned the highlands of modern-day Assam and Bangladesh in the east, the uplands of the Deccan Plateau in South India, the western edge of the Indus River Basin, northern Afghanistan in the northwest, and Kashmir in the north.

According to conventional wisdom, Babur, a Timurid chieftain from Transoxiana, established the Mughal Empire in 1526. He used assistance from the nearby Safavid and Ottoman Empires to defeat Ibrahim Lodi, the Sultan of Delhi, in the First Battle of Panipat and to engulf the

North Indian plains. However, some people date the Mughal imperial structure to 1600, under the reign of Akbar, Babur's grandson.

This imperial system persisted until 1720, not long after the passing of Aurangzeb, the final great emperor, who also saw the empire reach its greatest geographic size. Following the Indian Rebellion of 1857, the British Raj legally abolished the empire, which had been reduced to the area in and around Old Delhi by 1760.

A more effective, centralised, and standardised system of governance resulted from the Mughal Empire's equalisation and placation of the cultures and peoples it ruled through new administrative procedures and a diverse ruling class, despite the fact that it was founded and maintained by military conflict.

The third Mughal emperor Akbar established agricultural tariffs as the foundation of the empire's total riches. Peasants and artisans were forced to enter larger markets as a result of these taxes, which were paid in the strictly regulated silver coinage and represented well over half of a peasant cultivator's output.

The relative peace the empire enjoyed for much of the 17th century aided India's economic growth. The Mughal court benefited greatly from the growing demand for Indian raw and finished goods and the growing European presence in the Indian Ocean. Particularly under Shah Jahan's rule, the Mughal aristocracy's more ostentatious expenditures led to increased support for literature, painting, textiles, and architecture.

Agra Fort, Fatehpur Sikri, Red Fort, Humayun's Tomb, Lahore Fort, Shalamar Gardens, and the Taj Mahal—dubbed "the jewel of Muslim art in India, as well as one of the universally acclaimed masterpieces of the world's heritage"—are some of the Mughal UNESCO World Heritage Sites in South Asia.

Babur and Humayun (1526–1556)

Babur, a Central Asian king who ruled from 1526 to 1530, was descended from Genghis Khan on his mother's side and the Persianized Turco-Mongol conqueror Timur, the founder of the Timurid Empire, on his father's. Babur built the Mughal Empire. Babur's father was a member of the Mongol-born Turkicized Barlas tribe.

After being expelled from his Central Asian ancestral lands, Babur looked to India to fulfil his aspirations. He resided in Kabul before steadily advancing from Afghanistan across the Khyber Pass into India. Ibrahim Lodi, the Sultan of Delhi, was vanquished by Babur's army in the initial battle of Panipat in 1526.

Despite having fewer soldiers, he was nevertheless able to crush Ibrahim's army with guns and cannons, extending his rule to the middle of the Indo-Gangetic Plain. Following the conflict, Agra became the new centre of Mughal power.

With his local cavalry using typical flanking tactics, Babur's Timurid forces destroyed the unified Rajput armies of Rana Sanga of Mewar in the pivotal Battle of Khanwa, fought close to Agra a year later.

However, the new emperor was unable to solidify his achievements in India because of his obsession with battles and military exploits. His son, Humayun (1530–1556), sent into exile in Persia by the dissident Sher Shah Suri (1540–1545), exposed the empire's instability.

The Mughal and Safavid courts developed diplomatic relations during Humayun's exile in Persia, and the Mughal Empire's later restoration saw a rise in Persian cultural influence. After Humayun's victorious return from Persia in 1555, Mughal control was reinstated in some regions of India, but he passed away in an accident the following year.

Akbar to Aurangzeb (1556–1707)

In the Rajput Umarkot Fort, Akbar (r. 1556–1605) was born Jalal-ud-din Muhammad to Humayun and his Persian princess bride Hamida Banu Begum. Bairam Khan, a regent who assisted in the consolidation of the Mughal Empire in India, succeeded Akbar to the throne.

Akbar conquered the entire Indian subcontinent north of the Godavari River and expanded the empire in all directions. He established a new, obedient ruling class, a contemporary government, and promoted cultural advancements. He expanded his business dealings with European commercial firms.

India's economy became robust and stable, paving the way for economic growth and commercial expansion. Akbar established a new religion, Din-i-Ilahi, with strong traits of a ruler cult to address sociopolitical and cultural divisions within his empire while also permitting religious freedom at his court. Amid its golden period, he left his son in an externally stable state, but soon after, indications of political instability surfaced.

Jahangir (born Salim, 1605-1627) was born to Akbar and his Indian Rajput princess bride, Mariam-uz-Zamani. Salim Chishti, an Indian Sufi mystic, inspired the name Salim. He "became influenced by rival court cliques, neglected state affairs, and developed an opium addiction."

Jahangir set himself apart from Akbar by working hard to win over the authority of the Islamic establishment. He accomplished this, among other things, by giving far more madad-i-ma'ash (tax-free personal land revenue grants) to those who spiritually deserved or learnt than Akbar had. Unlike Akbar, Jahangir clashed with non-Muslim spiritual figures, most notably the Sikh guru Arjan, whose murder marked the beginning of numerous disputes between the Sikh community and the Mughal Empire.

Jahangir and his Rajput princess bride, Jagat Gosain, were the parents of Shah Jahan (1628-1658). The golden period of Mughal architecture began during his rule. The Taj Mahal is a prime example of the Mughal court's utmost magnificence during Shah Jahan's rule. However, the expenses of running the court started to outweigh the income. "The Golden Age of Mughal Architecture" was the moniker given to his rule. Shah Jahan expanded the Mughal Empire into the Deccan by putting an end to the Ahmadnagar Sultanate and requiring tribute from the Adil Shahis and Qutb Shahis.

In 1658, Shah Jahan's eldest son, the liberal Dara Shikoh, assumed the role of regent due to his father's illness. Dara, like his great-grandfather Akbar, promoted a syncretistic Hindu-Muslim civilisation. However, Aurangzeb (r. 1658–1707), Shah Jahan's younger son, took the throne with the help of Islamic orthodoxy. After defeating Dara in 1659, Aurangzeb had him put to death. Although Shah Jahan recovered from his illness, Aurangzeb kept him imprisoned until his death in 1666.

Aurangzeb oversaw the Mughal state's increasing Islamicization and expanded the empire's territory to its maximum size. He composed the Fatawa 'Alamgiri, a compilation of Islamic law, restored the jizya on non-Muslims, and promoted conversion to Islam. The Sikh community became militarised as a result of Aurangzeb's order to execute Tegh Bahadur, a Sikh guru.

From an imperial standpoint, local elites were incorporated into the king's idea of a network of common identity that would unite various communities across the empire under the Mughal emperor's rule. He oversaw battles in the Deccan starting in 1682, annexing the region's surviving Muslim strongholds, Bijapur and Golconda, but he also fought a protracted war there that severely damaged the empire. The Mughal treasury was heavily impacted by the battles, Aurangzeb's absence resulted in a sharp deterioration in governance, and stability and economic productivity in the Mughal Deccan fell precipitously.

Some historians contend that Aurangzeb's religious conservatism and intolerance threatened the stability of Mughal society, while others cast doubt on this, pointing out that he constructed Hindu temples, hired a disproportionately large number of Hindus in his imperial bureaucracy compared to his predecessors, and opposed prejudice against Shia Muslims and Hindus. Aurangzeb is regarded as the most controversial Mughal emperor. Emperor Aurangzeb is known to have implemented oppressive measures against non-Muslims in spite of these accusations. Following this shift, a significant uprising by the Marathas occurred, sparked by their leader Shivaji's unrelenting state-building in the Deccan.

Cultural and Administrative Achievements

Contributions to Art, Architecture, and Culture

Culture: The Mughal Empire significantly impacted South Asian history during the early modern and modern eras. Its cultural contributions in Bangladesh, India, Pakistan, and Afghanistan include:

- Unifying minor South Asian polities under centralised imperial administration.

- Merging Indian art with Persian literature.

- Developing Mughal apparel, jewellery, and fashion using elaborately patterned materials like velvet, silk, brocade, and muslin.

- Creating Mughlai cuisine, which combines elements of Central Asian, Iranian, and South Asian cooking.

- Introducing advanced waterworks and horticultural techniques through Mughal gardening in the Iranian style.

- Influencing the evolution of the Hindustani language by integrating Persian into Old Hindi.

- Shaping later Rajput and Sikh palatial architecture through advancements in Mughal and Indian architectural designs, with the Taj Mahal standing as a famous example.

- Introducing Turkish baths to the Indian subcontinent.
- Establishing Maktab schools, where young people were instructed in their native tongues in the Quran and Islamic law, including the Fatawa 'Alamgiri.
- Evolving Pehlwani technique of Indian wrestling, which combines Persian *varzesh-e bastani* with Indian *malla-yuddha*.
- Contributing to the evolution of instruments like the sitar and Hindustani classical music.

Customs: There are numerous accounts of lavish presents at the Mughal Empire's royal marriage procession. One such instance occurred during the marriage of Salim, the son of Emperor Akbar, and Raja Bhagwant Das, the ruler of Bijapur, and his daughter. As a dowry, Bhagwant Das gave them a hundred elephants, numerous horses, and numerous male and female slaves of Abyssinian, Caucasian, and indigenous Indian ancestry.

Architecture: The Mughals significantly influenced the Indian subcontinent by creating their own unique architectural style. In addition to absorbing more inspiration from Hindu architecture, this style was influenced by Iranian and Central Asian architecture, especially Timurid architecture and earlier Indo-Islamic architecture. Among other things, Mughal architecture features bulbous domes, ogive arches, meticulously planned and polished façades, and the use of marble and strong red sandstone for buildings.

In addition, William Dalrymple noted that an ice house building was in Delhi in the latter days of the Mughal conquest of the city in 1857. It is said that Emperor Shah Jahan built an ice house in Sirmaur, north of Delhi. The Taj Mahal, a UNESCO World Heritage Site regarded as "the jewel of Muslim art in India and one of the generally admired masterpieces of the world's heritage," is one of the many monuments constructed during the Mughal era by Muslim emperors, particularly Shah Jahan. It receives between 7 and 8 million unique visitors annually.

Art and literature: Iranian, Indian, Chinese, and Renaissance European stylistic and thematic aspects were all included in the Mughal creative legacy, primarily represented in painted miniatures and other luxury items. Because of the similarities between their Timurid customs and the Mughal love of Iranian art and calligraphy, Mughal rulers frequently imported Iranian bookbinders, illustrators, painters, and calligraphers from the Safavid court.

The Mughal emperors commissioned miniatures, first concentrating on large projects that illustrated books full of historical events and court life. Later, they added more single images for albums, with portraits and animal paintings demonstrating a deep appreciation for the peace and beauty of nature. Emperor Jahangir, for instance, hired talented artists like Ustad Mansur to depict exotic plants and animals in the realm realistically.

Epics like the Razmnama (a Persian version of the Hindu epic, the Mahabharata), historical memoirs or histories of the dynasty like the Baburnama and Akbarnama, and Tuzk-e-Jahangiri were among the literary works that Akbar and Jahangir ordered illustrated.

Exquisitely finished albums (muraqqa) embellished with artistic scenes and calligraphy adhered to pages with ornamental borders and then sealed with leather covers that were either painted and lacquered or stamped and gilded. Due in large part to his religious beliefs, Aurangzeb (1658–1707) was never a very passionate patron of art. He abandoned the opulence and formality of the court in 1668, and it is likely that he never again commissioned any paintings after that.

The third Mughal emperor, Akbar, established the majority of the bureaucratic, highly centralised government of the Mughal Empire. The emperor led the central administration, with four ministries directly below him. Under the direction of a diwan, the finance/revenue ministry was in charge of managing the empire's territorial revenues, calculating tax receipts, and allocating tasks based on this data.

The Mir Bakhshi, who oversaw military structure, messenger service, and the Mansabdari system, was the head of the military's (army/intelligence) ministry. The sadr as-sudr was the head of the ministry that handled legal and religious patronage; they also selected judges and oversaw stipends and charitable donations. Under the direction of the Mir Saman, another ministry was devoted to public works and the imperial household. The diwan was the most important of these ministers and usually served as the empire's wazir, or prime minister.

Administrative Divisions

A provincial governor known as a subadar oversaw each of the Subah, or provinces that made up the empire. Each suba had its own finance minister, sadr as-sudr, and bakhshi who answered directly to the central government instead of the subahdar, mirroring the structure of the central government at the province level. Sarkars, the administrative divisions of Subas, were further subdivided into parganas, which were clusters of villages. The local tax collector and a Muslim judge made up the Mughal government in the Pargana. The Mughal Empire's fundamental administrative unit was the pargana.

The Mughals' administrative divisions were dynamic. To improve administrative control and expand farming, territories were frequently reorganised and reconstructed. A sarkar might become a subah, for instance, and parganas were frequently passed from one sarkar to another. The division hierarchy was sometimes unclear, as an area could have several overlapping jurisdictions.

Geographically, administrative divisions were also ambiguous. The Mughal state lacked the resources and power to conduct thorough land surveys, so the boundaries of these divisions were not established, and no maps were produced. Instead, using more straightforward land surveys, the Mughals documented comprehensive data on every division to evaluate the region's potential for income.

The Mughal Empire used the Sunni Hanafi legal system. In its early years, it relied on Hanafi legal precedents that were passed down from the Delhi Sultanate, its predecessor. Among these were the Fatawa al-Tatarkhaniyya (religious rulings of the Emir Tatarkhan) and the al-Hidayah (The Finest Guide). During the height of the empire, Emperor Aurangzeb commissioned the Fatawa 'Alamgiri, a comprehensive system of Hanafi law tailored to the specific context of South Asia, serving as a primary source of reference for the Mughal Empire. Additionally, the Mughal Empire adopted Persian ideas of kingship, where the emperor was regarded as the highest authority on matters of law.

Factors Leading to the Decline of the Mughal Empire

After a century of expansion and wealth, the Mughal Empire fell apart quickly between 1707 and 1720 for a variety of reasons, which historians have described in great detail. Political instability was brought about at the centre by civil battles over the succession and a slew of short-lived, weak, and inept leaders.

During the 17th century, the Mughals seemed invincible, but after they were overthrown, their imperial overstretch became evident, and the situation was irreparable. Since they were still vying for permission from the Mughal authorities to open factories and trade in India, the ostensibly harmless European trading organisations, like the British East Indies Company, had nothing to do with the initial fall.

Financially speaking, the throne lost the money required to support its chief officers, the emirs (nobles), and their families. As the widely dispersed imperial officers lost faith in the central government and began making bargains with influential local leaders, the emperor lost power. The imperial army lost its will to fight after becoming mired in protracted, pointless conflicts with the more belligerent Marathas.

At last, there were a number of bloody political conflicts over who should hold the monarchy. Following Emperor Farrukhsiyar's execution in 1719, local Mughal successor states seized control of successive regions.

Bahadur Shah I, Aurangzeb's son, tried to restructure the government and overturned his father's religious ideas. But upon his passing in 1712, the Mughal dynasty descended into anarchy and bloody feuds. Four emperors took the throne in succession in 1719 alone, acting as head of state under the governance of the Sadaat-e-Bara, a brotherhood of nobles from the Indian Muslim caste, whose leaders, the Sayyid Brothers, were the de facto rulers of the empire.

The empire started disintegrating under Muhammad Shah's rule (1719–1748), and large areas of central India were turned over from the Mughals to the Marathas. Nizam-ul-Mulk, Asaf Jah I, pushed the Marathas to conquer central and northern India while the Mughals attempted to stifle his independence in the Deccan. The Sack of Delhi destroyed the last of the Mughal dynasty's prestige and authority, as well as the entire Mughal treasury, marking the end of Nader Shah's Indian campaign, which had earlier restored Iranian suzerainty over the majority of West Asia, the Caucasus, and Central Asia.

The massive armies the Mughals formerly used to impose their rule could no longer be funded. To gain control over their affairs, many of the empire's elites seceded to establish separate kingdoms. However, the Mughal Emperor was still regarded as the pinnacle of power and continued to receive lip homage. In addition to the Muslim elite, representatives of the Maratha, Hindu, and Sikh communities participated in the formal recognition of the emperor as India's ruler.

In the meantime, many regional polities under the Mughal Empire's growing fragmentation engaged the state and themselves in international hostilities, which only resulted in defeat and territorial loss during conflicts like the Bengal War and the Carnatic Wars. Shah Alam II (1759–1806), the Mughal Emperor, attempted in vain to stop the Mughal fall. Delhi was overrun by the Afghans, and the emperor had shamefully taken temporary sanctuary with the British to the east when the Afghans (headed by Ahmad Shah Durrani) defeated the Maratha Empire in the Third Battle of Panipat in 1761.

After retaking Delhi from the Rohillas in 1771, the Marathas formally assumed the role of the emperor's protector in 1784. This situation persisted until the Second Anglo-Maratha War, when the British East India Company safeguarded the Mughal dynasty in Delhi.

The British colonial era over the Indian subcontinent began in 1793 when the British East India Company abolished local rule (Nizamat) and assumed control of the old Mughal province of Bengal-Bihar. This lasted until 1858. By 1857, the East India Company controlled a sizable portion of what had been Mughal India. The final Mughal emperor, Bahadur Shah Zafar, was overthrown by the British East India Company and sent to Rangoon, Burma in 1858 following a humiliating defeat in the Indian Rebellion 1857, which he ostensibly commanded.

Chapter Ten

The Safavid Empire (1501-1736 CE)

The Founding of the Safavid Empire

The region that is now Iran has a rich and lengthy history. The area was practically at the centre of global trade and power for centuries. Those in that position were referred to as the Safavid Dynasty and the Safavid Empire. It lasted from 1502 until 1736. A description of the Safavid Empire would be incomplete without mentioning the leadership that the Safavid monarchs exercised in the fields of art, religion, and military affairs.

Exactly who were the Safavids? Furthermore, how did the Safavid Empire come to dominate? When Sheikh Safi od-Din Ardabili lived in the middle of the 1200s, the Safavid monarchs were a Sufi religious order based on Shia Islam. He established a religious order that progressively expanded over the ensuing centuries. During the 15th century, the Safavids established a religious community and a military force.

Due to theological disagreements, the Safavids eventually started a war against portions of modern-day Georgia and Turkey. After winning the war, the Safavids created a new empire and took governmental control of the area. Of course, this is a very short summary of a highly complex procedure. It is crucial to better understand a few particular tale points.

The Dynasty of Safavid: During their lengthy rule, the Safavids altered many aspects of the societies they overran to increase the size of their empire. In what ways did the Safavid Empire grow? The Safavid Empire, also referred to as a gunpowder empire, possessed considerable military might and authority over its surrounding areas. Additionally, it was able to successfully incorporate gunpowder weaponry into its army. A number of the previous Safavid rulers were exceptionally skilled in military planning.

Persian became most of the empire's lingua franca, or common tongue, since it was centred in Persia (now Iran). Turkish was the preferred language in Ismail I's court, but his descendants gradually changed the language. Even though the Safavid-controlled territories were home to a diverse population, the Persian identity spread throughout the kingdom.

Notwithstanding their death in 1736, they left behind a legacy that included the restoration of Iran as a hub for trade between the East and the West, the creation of an effective government and bureaucracy founded on "checks and balances," their innovative architectural designs, and their support of the arts. By making Twelver Shi*ism the official religion of Iran and extending Shia Islam throughout most of the Middle East, Central Asia, the Caucasus, Anatolia, the Persian Gulf, and Mesopotamia, the Safavids have also left their mark on modern times.

The Safavid Empire's Construction: The Safavid Empire is said to have been founded by Ismail I, who came to power in 1501. The region's religious landscape changed dramatically when he proclaimed himself Shah of Iran and established Twelver Shia Islam as the official state religion. A pivotal moment in Safavid history occurred during the Battle of Chaldiran in 1514 against the Ottoman Empire. Despite the Safavids' defeat, this conflict marked the boundaries of the two empires and demonstrated the Safavid kings' tenacity and resolve.

Ismail I. Safavid, Shah (r. 1501-24): The Safavids changed from being a religious movement to a political dynasty ruled by a shah instead of a sheikh during the reign of Ismail I (r. 1501-24). This was made possible by the Qizilbash, who completely obeyed their leader and even offered themselves as martyrs in his service since they believed that he was an incarnation of God. Esmaʿil, who was only 15 years old at the time, established Safavid governmental power in 1501 when Azerbaijan was taken. He declared Tabriz his capital, had coins made in his name, and proclaimed himself king.

Ismail suffered a severe loss at Chaldoran in August of 1514 at the hands of his Sunni Turkish adversary, the Ottoman Sultan Selim I. The Safavids then lost Baghdad, Diyarbakır, and Kurdistan in the ongoing war against the Sunnis, the Ottomans in the west, and the Uzbeks in the northeast, while Tabriz was constantly in danger. Under Ismail's eldest son, Shah Tahmasp I (1524–76), Iran significantly deteriorated, and under his inept successors, Turkmen incursions into the realm grew more frequent and unchecked.

Chaldoran Battle: In the early 16th century, two powerful empires fought for control of eastern Turkey, Iraq, and Greater Syria. The Ottoman Empire was on one side, with its capital at Constantinople (present-day Istanbul) and base in western Turkey. Opposing it was the Safavid Empire, led by Shah Ismail.

He started with a string of conquests in northwest Iran and Azerbaijan. Nine years later, Shah Ismail took control of both Baghdad and the Iranian plateau. Sultan Selim I faced the Safavids because of the Ottomans' imminent threat from the Safavid Empire's rapid growth. On August 23, 1514, the Safavids and Ottomans engaged in combat in Chaldoran after Ottoman forces routed the Turkic tribes in eastern Turkey.

With the aid of artillery technology, the Ottomans prevailed in the conflict, solidifying their hold on Iraq and Kurdistan. Their defeat surprised the Safavids, who mainly relied on cavalry and used very little artillery.

The crucial issue, however, was that the Battle significantly influenced how the present Middle East was formed. Because the Safavids could not seize control of eastern Turkey and Iraq, their defeat at Chaldoran prevented the creation of a great empire in the Middle East. The current borders between Iran, Turkey, and Iraq were formed as a result of this incident.

The Safavid Empire's Golden Age: Shah Abbas I's rule, which lasted from 1588 to 1629, is frequently regarded as the Safavid Empire's heyday. A number of reforms were put in place by Shah Abbas I to improve the central government, economy, and military. By relocating the capital to Isfahan, Shah turned it into a centre of trade, architecture, and culture. He oversaw the empire's unparalleled expansion in trade, especially along the Silk Road, and artistic flowering, making Isfahan one of the world's most beautiful cities.

Replacement of Capital: In 1598, Abbas the Great relocated the Safavid capital from Qazvin, which had seized Tabriz on the Ottoman border fifty years earlier, to Isfahan. Since Isfahan was situated in the middle of Persia, it was less susceptible to invasion than Tabriz or Qazvin. Abbas likewise decorated Isfahan, the capital of the Seljuks centuries before. Under Abbas, Isfahan rose to become one of the biggest cities in the world.

Religious and Cultural Impact

One of Shah Ismail's most significant choices was declaring Shi'ism, a branch of Islam that was then entirely alien to Iranian culture, the official religion. The Safavids began a robust campaign of force and persuasion to convert the then-dominantly Sunni populace. The religious council of wise men known as the Sunni ulama either departed or was assassinated.

The Safavids recruited experts from Shi'ite nations to create a new religious elite to advance Shi'ism. To coordinate this elite and ensure it carried out the Shah's wishes, they chose a representative (the Sadr). The government essentially used religious leaders as a tool.

The Safavids also made gifts to religious schools and shrines to further the spread of religion. Most cunning of all, they created a new class of rich religious aristocrats who owed the state everything by using land and money grants. In particular, the Safavids oppressed all religions, including Shi'ites with differing beliefs and Sunni Muslims. Sufi mystic societies were prohibited, and alien shrines were vandalised.

This was unexpected because the Safavids were sprung from a Sufi order and a type of Shi'ism they now outlawed. Additionally, they downplayed the significance of the Hajj (the journey to Mecca) and substituted it with a pilgrimage to Shi'ite sites.

Religion in the Safavid Empire – the Positives

In essence, the early Safavid Empire was a theocracy. Political and religious authority was inextricably linked, and the Shah himself embodied both. Soon after, the Empire's citizens enthusiastically accepted the new religion and fervently observed Shi'ite holidays. The most important was Ashura, which Shia Muslims observe to commemorate Husayn's (RA) passing.

Ali (RA) was revered as well. Shi'ism's philosophy and theology advanced significantly during the Safavid Empire since it was now a state religion and had significant educational institutions dedicated to it. Despite being motivated and inspired by a strong religious belief, the Safavid Empire quickly established a robust central government and administration that was secular in nature.

Culture and the Arts: Eastern Persia developed into a major cultural hub throughout the Safavid era. Paintings, metalwork, carpets, and textiles all achieved unprecedented levels of excellence during this time. Patronage had to come from the highest levels for art to be successful on this scale. The love of beauty was not the only reason behind this.

A large portion of early art was devoted to honouring the splendours of the former Iranian kingdom, implicitly validating the Safavids as the contemporary heirs to that country. The Safavids were frequently themselves artists. Shah Tahmasp painted, and Shah Ismail wrote poetry. Their support, which included setting up royal seminars for artists, fostered an environment conducive to the advancement of art.

Isfahan, the capital of Shah Abbas, is an outstanding example of the Safavid period's artistic accomplishments and affluence. Europeans, who had never seen anything like this at home, were awed by the parks, libraries, and mosques at Isfahan. It was known to the Persians as Nisf-e-Jahan, or "half the world," because to view it was to see half of the world. Isfahan rose to become one of the most beautiful cities in the world. With a population of one million, it was also one of the biggest during its peak, with 163 mosques, 48 religious institutions, 1801 stores, and 263 public baths.

Internal Conflicts and External Pressures Leading to the Decline of the Safavid Empire

In its early years, the Safavid Empire remained intact by conquering additional lands and defending them against the Ottoman Empire, its neighbour. However, the Ottoman danger to the Safavids diminished in the seventeenth century, initially decreasing the armed forces' effectiveness.

The Safavid Shahs grew complacent, corrupt, and decadent as a result of their main adversary remaining silent. In the eighteenth century, the Shahs were overthrown, and the first Islamic Republic in history was established by the Shia ulama, a religious council of wise men who had gained power. The ulama came up with the idea that the only person who could reign was a Mujtahid or someone who had lived a blameless life and was well-versed in Sharia or Quranic law.

In 1726, an Afghan faction overthrew the governing dynasty. Following the conquest, the Shia ulama and the new Afghan Shahs agreed on a separation of powers. In addition to having the authority to impose taxes and enact secular laws, the Afghan Shahs dominated the government and foreign policy. The ulama maintained authority over religious activities and applied Sharia, or Quranic law, to private and domestic affairs. Iran is still resolving issues related to governmental and spiritual authority separation.

But at this time, the Empire was falling apart and remained in ruins for the next two centuries. It was pillaged at will by feudal lords and bandit chiefs, further undermining the Empire, and people longed for stability and powerful central authority. With the rise of the Pahlavis (1925–79), the dynastic idea and a powerful central authority in Iran were reaffirmed. The second Pahlavi Shah's role and style were influenced by the early 20th-century oil discovery and the British and American interest in it. He was able to run a lavish and dishonest court thanks to his oil money.

Up until the 1970s, the ulama persisted in tolerating the nonreligious Shahs, but in 1979, they destroyed the monarchy. As a result, the Ayatollahs, the ulama's top leaders, came to wield authority. The challenge to the Shah's royal power by Ayatollah Khomeini validated a long-standing religious tradition in Iranian history and society. Internal conflict, poor leadership, problems with succession, and external pressures from nearby nations like the Ottomans and Afghan invaders all contributed to the Safavid Empire's downfall. The empire finally fell in the early 18th century due to these causes.

Chapter Eleven

Comparative Analysis and Legacy of Islamic Empires

Comparing Governance and Administration

The Islamic empires each devised unique systems of governance that reflected their cultural contexts and the challenges they faced. The Rashidun Caliphate, the earliest Islamic polity, emphasised a consultative model. The caliphs ruled as both spiritual and temporal leaders, with decisions guided by the Quran and the Sunnah. Governance during this period was marked by simplicity, justice, and a commitment to the welfare of the Muslim ummah. Despite its effectiveness, challenges such as tribal disputes and the rapid expansion of territories strained the administrative structure.

The Umayyad Caliphate shifted governance toward a centralised model, focusing on consolidating power. Capital cities such as Damascus served as administrative hubs. Provincial governors (walis) managed local affairs, and a complex bureaucracy emerged. However, the Umayyads' favouritism and perceived elitism often alienated non-Arab Muslims (mawali), creating significant dissent.

The Abbasid Caliphate refined this bureaucratic system, borrowing heavily from Persian administrative traditions. Baghdad became a centre of governance, and viziers played crucial roles in policy and administration. The Abbasids' emphasis on inclusivity, particularly in employing diverse ethnic groups, helped stabilise their vast territories. Nevertheless, their reliance on military slave elites and regional governors sometimes led to fragmentation.

The Ottoman Empire's governance model represented an evolution of Islamic administration, integrating Islamic law with a pragmatic and centralised system. The sultans wielded absolute power, supported by the diwan (Imperial Council) and an efficient bureaucracy. A notable feature was the millet system, which allowed religious minorities autonomy in personal and community affairs. This inclusivity helped maintain stability but occasionally sowed divisions between various groups.

The Mughal Empire's governance emphasised cultural syncretism and local autonomy. Akbar's policy of Sulh-e-Kul (peace for all) facilitated cooperation among diverse religious and ethnic communities. The mansabdari system created a merit-based administration, but excessive decentralisation and later administrative inefficiencies contributed to the empire's decline.

Each empire faced challenges, including succession disputes, regional rebellions, and external invasions. Yet, their administrative legacies persist, shaping modern governance in various parts of the Islamic world.

Cultural and Scientific Contributions

The Islamic empires profoundly influenced art, science, and culture, leaving legacies that resonate globally. Cultural Achievements: Islamic architecture flourished across empires, with iconic structures like the Dome of the Rock (Umayyads), the Alhambra (Nasrid Granada), the Hagia Sophia's transformation (Ottomans), and the Taj Mahal

(Mughals). Calligraphy, geometric patterns, and arabesque designs became defining features of Islamic art. The Abbasid period, particularly during the caliphate of Harun al-Rashid, saw the establishment of Baghdad as a cultural and intellectual hub. The House of Wisdom attracted scholars who translated Greek, Persian, and Indian texts, preserving and expanding ancient knowledge.

Scientific Contributions: The Islamic Golden Age, primarily under the Abbasids, witnessed remarkable advancements in mathematics, astronomy, medicine, and engineering. Al-Khwarizmi developed algebra, while Ibn Sina's "Canon of Medicine" remained a standard medical text for centuries. Astronomers like al-Biruni and al-Tusi made significant contributions, influencing later European scientific thought.

The Ottomans excelled in cartography and military technology, with figures like Piri Reis producing detailed maps. The Mughals advanced metallurgy and agronomy, enhancing economic productivity. These empires emphasised education, establishing madrasas and libraries and fostering intellectual growth that bridged cultures and eras.

Lasting Impact on the Modern Islamic World

The legacies of the Islamic empires continue to shape contemporary societies, particularly in governance, culture, and education. The Rashidun's emphasis on justice and consultation remains a cornerstone of Islamic political thought. The Ottomans' millet system prefigured modern pluralistic governance models, emphasising coexistence among diverse communities.

Culturally, the artistic and architectural innovations of these empires influence modern design. For instance, the Mughal aesthetic is evident in South Asian art and urban planning. Similarly, the Abbasids' intellectual endeavours laid the groundwork for modern science and philosophy. Their preservation of ancient texts ensured the survival of knowledge that underpins contemporary education.

Contemporary Societal Influences

Modern Islamic societies continue to draw inspiration from these empires. Rashidun's egalitarian principles resonate with movements advocating social justice. The Umayyads' and Abbasids' achievements in governance inform administrative reforms in several Muslim-majority countries.

Cultural festivals, architectural preservation, and educational curricula emphasise the rich heritage of these empires. Turkey's restoration of historic sites celebrates the Ottoman legacy. Similarly, South Asia honours the Mughal influence through its cuisine, language, and art.

The Abbasids' scientific ethos inspired renewed focus on STEM education in many Islamic nations. Moreover, the empires' emphasis on trade and cultural exchange encouraged global cooperation in a modern context.

The Islamic empires were not only political entities but also cultural and intellectual beacons. Their governance models, artistic achievements, and scientific contributions left indelible marks on the world. Comparing their governance and cultural legacies reveals their strengths and challenges. Their enduring impact shapes modern Islamic societies, fostering a sense of pride and providing a blueprint for future progress.

Chapter Twelve

Conclusion

The history of Islamic dynasties is a rich and complex narrative reflecting human ambition's transformative power when guided by faith, intellect, and a shared cultural ethos. From the early days of the Rashidun Caliphate to the magnificent reigns of the Ottomans, Mughals, and Safavids, these empires carved a profound legacy that extends far beyond their geographical boundaries. Their stories are filled with remarkable achievements in governance, science, art, and cultural integration, as well as the inherent challenges of managing vast, diverse domains. This tapestry of history is a testament to the resilience and ingenuity of human civilisations.

The Rashidun Caliphate, as the foundational Islamic dynasty, set the stage for what would become a transformative era in global history. Emerging after the Prophet Muhammad's (PBUH) passing, the Rashidun Caliphate exemplified principles of justice, governance, and cultural inclusivity. Their leadership expanded Islamic territories and established administrative systems that emphasised fairness and efficiency. This early governance model became the blueprint for subsequent dynasties, blending spiritual principles with practical statecraft.

Following the Rashidun Caliphate, the Umayyads took the helm, marking a period of unprecedented territorial expansion. Stretching from the Iberian Peninsula to Central Asia, the Umayyads introduced a centralised administrative structure that facilitated communication and trade across vast regions. Their emphasis on infrastructure development, including road networks and postal systems, enhanced connectivity and laid the groundwork for cultural exchange. The Umayyads also fostered the growth of cities like Damascus and Cordoba, which became vibrant centres of knowledge and learning.

The Abbasid Caliphate succeeded the Umayyads, ushering in a golden age of intellectual and cultural flourishing. Centred in Baghdad, the Abbasids cultivated a thriving atmosphere of scholarship and innovation. The establishment of institutions like the House of Wisdom symbolised their commitment to knowledge, drawing scholars from diverse backgrounds to translate and expand upon works of science, philosophy, and literature. Figures such as al-Khwarizmi, the father of algebra, and Ibn Sina, a pioneer in medicine, emerged during this period, leaving legacies that continue to shape modern disciplines.

Parallel to the Abbasids, the Islamic world witnessed the rise of regional dynasties such as the Fatimids, Ayyubids, and Seljuks. Each of these dynasties brought unique contributions to the Islamic tapestry. The Fatimids, known for their architectural marvels like Cairo's Al-Azhar Mosque, emphasised the arts and education. The Ayyubids, under the leadership of Salah al-Din (Saladin), exemplified chivalry and unity during the Crusades, earning respect from both allies and adversaries. On the other hand, the Seljuks revitalised Islamic art and architecture, leaving behind iconic structures like the mosques of Isfahan.

The Ottoman Empire, one of the most enduring Islamic dynasties, stands as a monumental chapter in this history. Spanning over six centuries, the Ottomans mastered the art of governance by blending diverse traditions and cultures within their expansive territory. Their administrative innovations, such as the millet system, allowed religious and ethnic communities to coexist while maintaining autonomy. The architectural genius of Sinan reflected in masterpieces like the Suleymaniye Mosque and the cultural patronage of figures like Suleiman the Magnificent further underscored their commitment to art, science, and governance.

In South Asia, the Mughal Empire represented another pinnacle of Islamic civilisation. Renowned for their architectural grandeur and cultural synthesis, the Mughals left an indelible mark on the Indian subcontinent. Iconic structures like the Taj Mahal are not only testaments to their artistic vision but also symbols of their ability to harmonise Persian, Indian, and Islamic aesthetics. The Mughals fostered a rich literary and artistic tradition, with rulers like Akbar promoting tolerance and intellectual curiosity through initiatives like the Din-i-Ilahi, a syncretic belief system that sought unity among diverse faiths.

The Safavid Empire, centred in Persia, demonstrated the dynamic interplay between religion and governance. By establishing Twelver Shi'ism as the state religion, the Safavids created a distinct cultural and religious identity that continues to influence Iran today. Their contributions to art and architecture, such as the stunning Imam Mosque in Isfahan, are celebrated for their intricate designs and vibrant colours. The Safavids also played a pivotal role in facilitating trade along the Silk Road, connecting East and West and fostering economic prosperity.

These dynasties shared common threads that defined their success and challenges. Their emphasis on education and knowledge production fostered an environment of innovation that enriched humanity's intellectual heritage. Advances in astronomy, medicine, mathematics, and engineering not only served their own societies but also laid the foundation for the European Renaissance. The intricate patterns of Islamic art, the poetic depth of Persian literature, and the architectural grandeur of their monuments continue to inspire awe and admiration.

Trade played a crucial role in the prosperity of Islamic dynasties. Cities like Baghdad, Damascus, Istanbul, and Delhi became bustling hubs of commerce and culture, attracting merchants, scholars, and artisans from across the world. This interaction of ideas and goods facilitated cultural synthesis, fostering an environment where diversity thrived. The principles of tolerance and inclusivity within these societies enabled different faiths, languages, and traditions to coexist, creating a harmonious blend of cultures.

Despite their achievements, these dynasties also faced significant challenges. The complexities of managing vast, diverse territories often led to internal strife and fragmentation. Succession disputes, external invasions, and economic pressures tested their resilience. However, even in decline, their cultural and intellectual contributions remained influential, serving as beacons of inspiration for subsequent generations.

Reflecting on the legacies of these Islamic dynasties reveals valuable lessons for contemporary society. Their ability to balance tradition with innovation, unity with diversity, and governance with cultural enrichment provides timeless insights into the dynamics of leadership and the potential for human civilisations to thrive. These empires remind us that the pursuit of knowledge and justice can transcend boundaries, fostering a shared human experience rooted in mutual respect and collaboration.

In a world grappling with challenges such as polarisation, inequality, and cultural disconnection, the stories of these dynasties offer hope and guidance. Their emphasis on education, cultural exchange, and celebrating diversity underscores the importance of building inclusive and progressive societies. They teach us that human potential is boundless when guided by principles of justice, intellect, and faith.

The legacies of these dynasties are more than relics of the past; they are vibrant threads in the fabric of global history, connecting us to a tradition of excellence and innovation. May their stories continue to enlighten and inspire, urging us to draw from the wisdom of the past as we navigate the challenges of the present and chart a course toward a brighter future. The impact of these Islamic dynasties endures a timeless tribute to the resilience, creativity, and transformative power of human ambition.

Find Out More

Website: www.barakahinbusiness.com

Socials: @barakahinbusiness

If you enjoyed this book, kindly leave a review to help expand our reach so others may benefit also.

www.ingramcontent.com/pod-product-compliance
Lightning Source LLC
Chambersburg PA
CBHW052212090526
44584CB00019BA/3053